BORDERLANDS

BORDERLANDS

The Heritage of the Lower Río Grande through the Art of

José Cisneros

EDINBURG • TEXAS

Copyright © 1998 by the Hidalgo County Historical Museum

ISBN 1-888594-03-9

Artwork by José Cisneros

Authors / Dr. Félix D. Almaráz, Jr.; Dr. Hubert J. Miller; Tom Fort; Rachael Freyman
Editor / Jackie Nirenberg
Book and cover design / Erren Seale
Print coordination and color work / Bob Carter

Hidalgo County Historical Museum
121 E. McIntyre
Edinburg, Texas 78539

(956) 383-6911   FAX (956) 381-8518

All rights reserved.
No part of this publication may be reproduced without expressed written consent
of the Hidalgo County Historical Museum.

Printed In Canada

*Dedicated to the generations of peoples
who shaped the ever-changing borderlands, and to
José Cisneros, the artist who so brilliantly brings them to life.*

CONTENTS

9   Preface

11   José Cisneros: An Artist in Pursuit of a Star
by Félix D. Almaráz, Jr.

17   Four Centuries of Shared Experience in the Borderlands
by Hubert J. Miller & Félix D. Almaráz, Jr.

43   The José Cisneros Collection

155   Index of Illustrations

156   Suggested Reading

157   Acknowledgements

158   Preserving Our Borderland Heritage

159   The Hidalgo County Historical Museum

PREFACE

History is, fundamentally, a marriage of perspectives. At its best, it is a synthesis of eyewitness accounts, carefully sifted to reveal kernels of truth. There are times when the search for those truths can be more challenging than others—when documentation is limited, and when a tradition of oral history is great. Researchers are often faced with varying, if not outright conflicting, accounts of how a sequence of significant events unfolded. The result is a lively and spirited debate in which a colorful cast of characters, and a fluctuating set of physical, geographical and temporal references figure prominently. Such is the case with the magnificent history of the lower Río Grande of Texas. Widely-varying documentation, word-of-mouth accounts, and a plethora of cultural perspectives provide plenty of academic fodder to fuel the debate for decades to come.

This book, however, is not an academic exercise. Rather, it attempts to bring a fascinating history to life through both art and narrative. *Borderlands: The Heritage of the Lower Río Grande through the Art of José Cisneros* is a celebration of the work of a renowned artist, José Cisneros, and the unique collection of hand-colored pen-and-ink drawings he created expressly for the Hidalgo County Historical Museum in Edinburg, Texas. The drawings illustrate, in stunning detail, the early native inhabitants, the Spanish explorers, the *ganaderos* and *vaqueros*, the military men and the generations of brave pioneers who made this region what it is today. An eloquent forward by Dr. Félix D. Almaráz, an historical introduction by Drs. Hubert J. Miller and Félix D. Almaráz, and informative commentaries on each drawing by Museum staff members Tom Fort and Rachael Freyman provide an excellent backdrop for the collection of works.

Cisneros' mastery of the traditional art of pen-and-ink illustration is in itself a tribute to days gone by. Each of his drawings is an invitation to experience history in glorious color and detail. Each stroke of his pen brings to life the story of those who left their indelible mark on this rugged land, and each brilliant detail is a testament to the artist's passion for borderland history—a passion he shares with so many others.

José Cisneros: An Artist in Pursuit of a Star

by Félix D. Almaráz, Jr.

Thirty years ago, José Cisneros took two giant leaps of faith in quick succession. The first leap occurred in the autumn of 1968, coinciding with the annual meeting of the Western History Association in Tucson, Arizona. A few years before, John Porter Bloom, an influential member of the new organization, had invited Cisneros to design a logo for the WHA. After considerable reflection, José created a wagon wheel, accented by an Indian arrow, with the association's name prominently displayed around the rim. The logo depicted migration, adversity, and renewal in the great American West.

Aware of this contribution to the organization, Harwood Hinton, then at the University of Arizona, encouraged José to prepare an exhibit for the 1968 WHA meeting in Tucson. Accordingly, the artist reserved two meeting rooms in the Pioneer Hotel, site of the convention, where he anxiously mounted an attractive array of about thirty original drawings, each an exquisite pen-and-ink rendition of life in the borderlands, ranging in theme from the conquest of Mexico to the advent of the American cowboy. In the hotel lobby, José attached a placard to an easel, inviting historians to view his exhibit, *Riders of the Borderlands*. The cadre of historians who attended the exhibit expressed admiration and approval, not only of the artist's remarkable talent, but also of his profound knowledge in the subject matter that his drawings reflected. After the convention, these scholars, the original *aficionados* (enthusiasts), returned to their respective communities, praising and promoting the work of José Cisneros among librarians, editors, publishers, art dealers, museum directors, gallery owners, and private collectors.

Not long after the Tucson exhibit, Cisneros initiated a second leap of faith as an artist. Through the friendly intercession of L. Tuffly Ellis, Eldon S. Branda, and the late Joe B. Frantz, all affiliated with the Texas State Historical Association, the artist applied for a Dobie Paisano Fellowship, awarded semi-annually by the Board of Regents of the University of Texas System. Ironically, before selecting Cisneros as the 1969 Paisano laureate, some regents, preferring to support writers with academic credentials, expressed strong reservations about awarding the honor to an unknown artist.

Leaving behind the security of regular employment with the El Paso City Lines, a public transportation system, José resolved to devote his time and talent exclusively to perfecting a technique in illustrating the historical sweep of a vast cultural region. With great trepidation, tempered by the award of the fellowship, the artist retreated into the secluded and beautiful environment of the University of Texas' Paisano Ranch, Dobie's former home near Austin, to create a legacy that earned for him wide acclaim as a serious interpreter of the pioneer experience in the northern frontier of colonial Mexico.

Riders of the Border, a small publication featuring a cavalcade of Cisneros' artistic renditions produced at Paisano during a six-month standard of relentless dedication, became a partial record of a stellar showcase of his work exhibited in Austin, San Antonio, Mexico City, Los Angeles, Lubbock, Harlingen, and Edinburg. Without a doubt, Cisneros emerged from the Paisano experience to become the Fellowship Program's most productive scholar/artist in residence, a hallmark achievement that amazed the Board of Regents.

A salient characteristic that evolved from these early exhibitions was the impeccable detail José applied to the riders, especially their costumes and equipment, and to the graceful movement of the horses. An observant critic concluded that Cisneros created the horses first, and then introduced the riders as an afterthought. José later clarified the decision that changed his career: "I made a commitment to follow their hoof prints along and across the land."

In recognition of the artist's multiple contributions to literature, Westerners International, a world-wide organization of persons enamored of the American West, in April 1998, proclaimed José Cisneros "A Living Legend." Earlier, on June 28, 1997, the Western Writers of America presented the Owen Wister Award to Cisneros. At the ceremony in Cheyenne, Wyoming, Preston Lewis acknowledged that the Wister Award, created in memory of the author of *The Virginian,* was the highest honor the group bestowed upon an individual. As presiding officer of the Western Writers of America, Lewis expressed a few of the sentiments held by a legion of Cisneros' admirers.

He has been honored by presidents and governors, popes and professors. Despite his many honors and accolades, he remains to this day a humble man who taught himself to read and to draw. Because his formal education is modest, he does not consider himself an educated man, but I would disagree for an educated [person] always works to expand his mind.

José has done that throughout his lifetime and I would submit there is not a better educated person in this room. And we in this room — all lovers of history and the West — are richer for his education because he has taught us much.

Six months prior to the announcement of the Wister Award, M. A. Maier, a free-lance writer for *SouthwestArt,* asked José to explain the secret of his growing success. "To improve my art, I have to keep learning," Cisneros replied. "I have forced myself to do better, and my art has grown with me."

Indicative of that constant perfection of a God-given talent, in the spring of 1998, gentle artist José Cisneros received a supreme tribute from the State of Texas in the form of a reception and dinner in Austin, hosted by Governor and Mrs. George W. Bush. A cross-section of José's widening circle of family, friends, and admirers congregated at the Governor's Mansion to celebrate his life and achievements. Lauding José as "a great El Paso treasure," Governor Bush avowed he was "honored to call him a friend."

José Cisneros' quest for a star began on April 18, 1910, in the hamlet of San Miguel de las Bocas (subsequently renamed Villa Ocampo), Durango, Mexico. Born to Fernando Cisneros and Juanita Barragán de Cisneros on the eve of the Mexican Revolution, the infant José remained oblivious for several years to the turbulence that uprooted families wherever opposing armies contested the land space. For several years the homeless Cisneros family wandered like gypsy moths across northern Mexico.

Experienced as a resourceful craftsman (carpenter, musician, barber, blacksmith and railroad contruction worker), Fernando took the family to Dorado, Chihuahua, in search of gainful employment, but all he found was work as a carpenter. Without proper tools and training, Fernando improvised by pursuing a craft of constructing chests, reminiscent of an old Spanish tradition, joined together by wooden pegs instead of nails.

During these difficult years, José taught himself to read. With the help of a primer textbook, *Silabario Metódico,* he discovered the elements of phonics. By systematically memorizing the sounds of letters and their combinations, the youngster crashed into the world of reading. An uncle who resided in the town of Valle de Allende, in southern Chihuahua, delighted in the news that eleven-year-old José could read. He took his precocious nephew home and sent him to school for three years.

In the peaceful environment of Valle de Allende, José learned that in the sixteenth century, when the town was known as San Bartolomé, Antonio de Espejo and Juan de Oñate organized their expeditions in that community for the final thrust into New Mexico. A dynamic teacher, endowed with an extraordinary gift of story-telling, introduced the students to history. Through the medium of word pictures the distant past jumped into José's consciousness. With drama and vivid imagination the teacher mesmerized the class with narrations of dominant personalities in history, together with picturesque versions of their colorful attire and battery of equipment. That remarkable teacher, whose name receded from the student's memory, ignited José's inquisitive mind with stories about horses, their prancing movements, including a precise nomenclature of the equipment they carried.

The three years of formal instruction, filled with memorable experiences, passed rapidly. José compiled a collection of equestrian illustrations, appropriated from Sunday supplements in the newspapers delivered to Valle de Allende. One publication from Mexico City, *El Hogar* (the home), featured a juvenile section that caught José's attention. The editor of *El Hogar* invited budding artists and writers to submit manuscripts for evaluation. José, now fourteen years old, mailed a short essay entitled "Un Viaje" (a journey), complete with a line-drawn likeness of himself. When published, "Un Viaje" described José's own journey through school in quest of a star. In January, 1925, *El Hogar* published José's second initiative, "Primavera" (springtime), in which the young artist used minute detail in creating images of flowers, colors, and clouds.

Later in 1925, grateful for his uncle's benevolence, José rejoined his family. In Ciudad Juárez, José's father Fernando found steady employment. José secured a student passport to enroll at the Lydia Patterson Institute in El Paso, where he dedicated himself to studying English. To defray living expenses and tuition, he swept halls and classrooms. In addition, to earn supplemental income for his schooling, José delivered morning and evening editions of local newspapers. Eventually, with the help of the director of Lydia Patterson, the student applied for a work passport that legally allowed him to seek employment during after-school hours to earn extra money to contribute to the family in Ciudad Juárez.

In between classes, newspaper deliveries, and occasional odd jobs, Cisneros expanded his collection of illustrations gleaned from magazines and newspapers. He also reserved time to work on his own drawings. Sadly, José's artistic initiatives failed to win the approval of members of his family, who equated his drawings to *monitos* (worthless doodles). Disappointed but not discouraged, Cisneros continued to practice his art.

In a technical sense, José emigrated to the United States in 1927, although he maintained dual residency during his parents' declining years. Separated from the joy of daily instruction, the former student discovered the El Paso Public Library as an alternative source of learning. Guided in his selection of books by Maud Durlin Sullivan, the library director, José continued to study and to draw. Gradually, whenever he could afford the small luxury, he purchased books of art for his own library.

In the 1930s, José ventured into Mexican journals with his art. Admittedly the contributions failed to generate financial reward for the struggling artist, but the exposure of his work to wider audiences adequately compensated him. His illustrations appeared frequently in *Revista de Revistas, Vida Mexicana,* and *Todo*. Closer to home, a new publication, *El León Juarense*, extended an opportunity for José to experiment with a newspaper series, "Apuntes Históricos" (historical notes), which he wrote and illustrated. Through this journalistic venue Cisneros developed and perfected historical themes, all associated with El Paso del Norte, that later became signature pieces of his art. Beginning with the travels of Alvar Núñez Cabeza de Vaca and his three companions (1536), the cavalcade progressed with the Rodríguez-Sánchez Chamuscado expedition (1581), the *entrada* of Antonio de Espejo (1582), Don Juan de Oñate and the Founding of New Mexico (1598), and the establishment of Mission Nuestra Señora de Guadalupe (1659). Cisneros concluded the series with a description of colonial life in the region in 1750. In the series, the artist, dependent upon available research materials, manifested effective control of costumes, backgrounds, details, and, in some cases, equestrian skills.

Encouraged by the popular success of his Mexican publications, in 1937 Cisneros advanced toward the first defining moment in his career as an artist. Tom Lea, a renowned El Paso artist, accepted a commission to paint a mural in the lobby of the United States Courthouse, depicting a confluence of cultures in the region. When not at work, Cisneros watched as Lea enhanced the details in his mural. Finally, José mustered enough courage to interrupt Lea's work to show him a portfolio of illustrations. On a scrap of tracing paper the muralist scrawled a note to the librarian who earlier had assisted José in his program of self-study. Assessing Cisneros' drawings as "EXCEPTIONAL," Lea advised Mrs. Sullivan to examine the illustrations and, perhaps, to consider exhibiting them. "This fellow has some stuff," Tom Lea concluded.

The encounter with Lea resulted in Cisneros' first exhibition in El Paso. For this special event, held at the El Paso Public Library in March 1938, José compiled forty illustrations, the majority of which were pen-and-ink drawings interspersed with a few sketches in color. A favorable review by a critic, published in the El Paso *Herald,* attracted more patrons to the library which extended the exhibit for another week. Before the month ended, another complimentary review by poet Heriberto García-Rivas, who described Cisneros as "young and Mexican," signifying "dynamic and artistic by heritage," inspired the directors of the Centro Escolar Benito Juárez to invite José to transport his *Exposición de Arte* across the Río Grande to inaugurate a new auditorium. The event in Ciudad Juárez, featuring Cisneros' exhibit as a centerpiece, evolved into a gala celebration, highlighted by artistic dancing, solo and twin piano recitals, vocal renditions, and recitations of poetry.

The propitious meeting with Tom Lea produced another trajectory in Cisneros' career as an artist. Lea, who had collaborated for several years with Carl Hertzog, eminent book designer and typographer, envisioned that José would find a similar outlet for his projects. In 1938 a small window of opportunity opened for Cisneros to work with Hertzog. Several organizations formed an alliance to prepare memorials in honor of deceased Rabbi Martin Zielonka. The documents, printed by Hertzog, featured illuminated initials in red ink created by José Cisneros. Several years elapsed, however, before Hertzog, Lea, and Cisneros worked on a major project.

In 1939, Cisneros divided his time between working

at a department store, drawing in his spare time, and studying the work of prominent artists. That same year his father died, leaving José to assume responsibility for the welfare of his aging mother. Sorrow in losing a parent soon changed into rejoicing when José met Vicenta Madero, who became his loyal wife and constructive critic. Together they reared a family of five daughters and a niece, all of whom became ardent supporters of José's determination to succeed as an artist. One day Cisneros marshalled the courage to confess to Tom Lea that he had been born color-blind! Pensive for a moment, Lea advised José not to worry because in his hands he possessed a world in black-and-white. Gradually, he learned to confront the handicap by asking Vicenta to label the colored pencils. On some occasions the daughters suggested specific colors to accent the various components in the more intricate pen-and-ink creations. The issue of José's color blindness was not devoid of personal pain. When he reported for work as a spray painter in the maintenance department of the El Paso City Lines, a supervisor, dismayed with José's inability to distinguish colors, predicted he would be a disaster in that line of labor, but with effort he could become a master bricklayer! Again, through sheer determination, meritorious work, and wholesome humor, José managed to control the disability and earned promotion to foreman of the paint division.

During the 1940s, especially in the war years, José's artistic growth remained static. In the meantime, he studied the styles and techniques of accomplished artists. Among the artists who influenced José's development were Alejandro Sírio of Argentina, Ernesto García Cabral of Mexico, and Norman Rockwell and Howard Pyle of the United States. As much as Cisneros admired the techniques and achievements of the four artists, he accepted the reality of finding and improving his own unique style of expression. A manifestation of this search for style was the calligraphy that the artist learned to execute so elegantly. As with reading, José taught himself to draw the letters, a slow, methodical, laborious process. Quite by accident he found a book on calligraphy that illustrated how certain strokes required deliberate systematic operations. By improving his own technique, Cisneros uncovered the beauty of calligraphic effects which he easily transferred to his art.

After the war, Cisneros and Hertzog found ample opportunities to collaborate on projects. In 1946, Hertzog accepted a commission to produce a commemorative program for National Music Week in El Paso. Searching for a solution to enhance unused advertising spaces in the layout, Hertzog decided to fill the gaping blanks with biographical cameos of American composers. For uniformity of style, Hertzog persuaded José to prepare the sketches of the composers. This program represented the first in a long line of cooperative ventures between the two friends. Over the years their collaboration resulted in a variety of quality publications: *Across Aboriginal America: The Journey of Three Englishmen Across Texas* (1947), *The Red River Valley, Then and Now* (1948), *The Journey of Fray Marcos de Niza* (1949), and *The Spanish Heritage of the Southwest* (1951). As director of Texas Western Press on the campus of Texas Western College, Hertzog invited José to create original illustrations for a multitude of books. The long alliance with Carl Hertzog terminated slowly with the printer's semi-retirement from Texas Western Press in 1972. During this period of great productivity, José Cisneros became a naturalized citizen of the United States in 1948. Although Carl Hertzog attended the ceremony, Justice Department authorities disqualified him as José's official sponsor on a technicality that he had been born in Lyons, France. Hence, a foreman and a worker of the El Paso City Lines filled the void as Cisneros' sponsors of record.

Cisneros' friendship with Tom Lea and Carl Hertzog led to a number of challenging projects, including the design of a seal for Texas Western College. Later when the Board of Regents changed the name of the institution to the University of Texas at El Paso, Cisneros modified the initial design to accommodate the requirements for a new seal. Cisneros' frequent illustrations in books produced by Texas Western Press widened the artist's scope of contacts which resulted in increased demand for his creations. Still, public recognition of his art remained confined to the western rim of Texas by the Río Grande. Suddenly, however, the prestige of the WHA exhibit and the Paisano fellowship widened the horizon for the gentle artist of El Paso.

After each exposition the requests for Cisneros originals or prints significantly increased. Whereas in the struggling years, the artist would complete an illustration in four evenings, now the growing demand required that he reevaluate his work schedule. For a few more years he maintained the balancing act of full-time work and part-time art until he retired from the El Paso City Lines in 1973.

Besides books, which represented the main venue, José's artistic creations sequentially extended to carved statues for churches, stained-glass windows, bookplates, posters, maps, decorative carvings, commemorative medallions, ceramic tiles, leaflets, letterheads, and certificates. His book illustrations quietly invaded the editorial rooms of east-coast publishing firms, typified by Random House and Alfred A. Knopf.

In the seniority of life when most retired persons rush into planned inactivity, José Cisneros firmly resisted the temptation to rest on his multiple laurels. For a while the grief of losing his wife Vicenta and oldest daughter Inez interrupted his work. Yet, like a biblical patriarch he kept the Cisneros family together during their sorrow. In the process of finding consolation after Vicenta's death José traveled to Spain, land of his dreams, where he spent hours admiring priceless treasures in art galleries. On a second visit to Europe, accompanied by his daughters, José truly enjoyed the pleasure of introducing them to the splendors of Spain.

Back in El Paso, thankful for the chance to devote himself completely to his beloved monitos (now wholly appreciated as valuable pieces of art), Don José has continued to pursue his star with grace and dignity *on the job*. Convinced he has not reached the pinnacle of success and creativity, José Cisneros, incomparable citizen of the borderlands, declared recently, "Usually the best picture I have is the one I haven't done yet."

+ *The author gratefully acknowledges the assistance of John O. West, Preston Lewis, Albert T. Lowman, M. A. Maier, José Cisneros, and Right Reverend Monsignor Francis J. Smith in the composition of this essay. The steadfast support of Dolores Marie Cardona de Almaráz is lovingly appreciated.*

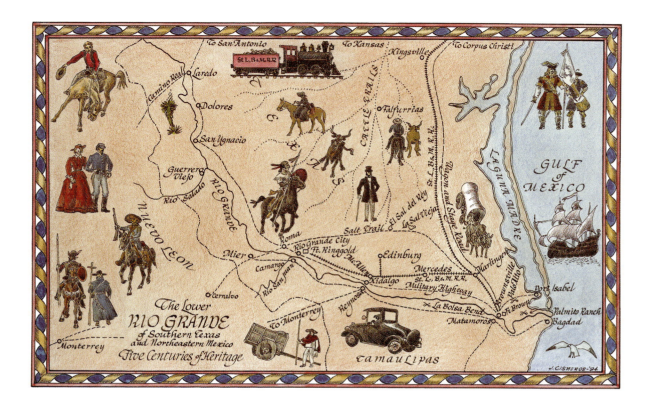

Four Centuries of Shared Experience in the Borderlands

by Dr. Hubert J. Miller &
Dr. Félix D. Almaráz, Jr.

The lower Río Grande region, throughout much of its history, was an integral part of a larger area known as the *Seno Mexicano*. The area roughly included the present-day Mexican state of Tamaulipas and the southern triangle of Texas, with a boundary line running northward from Laredo to the upper Río Nueces, then following the river to Corpus Christi, and from there along the coast to Brownsville.

Prior to the arrival of the Spaniards in the early 1500s, Native Americans inhabited the Seno Mexicano. Little is known about these inhabitants, except what has been learned through Spanish accounts. Unfortunately, these reports, greatly colored by European perceptions, leave many questions unanswered about these early people. Yet the contacts between the Native Americans and the Spaniards initiated a shared experience in the Seno Mexicano. And just 100 years after Spain's colonization of the area in the mid-1700s, the historical process of shared experience continued—this time with North Americans.

As is true for many border areas throughout the world, the lower Rio Grande Valley serves as a meeting place of peoples. The river unites these peoples rather than separating them. The meeting of peoples and sharing of experiences has been painful at times, but overall it has been rewarding.

Pre-Columbian Peoples

Before the arrival of the Spaniards, there were probably some 80 different Indian tribes inhabiting the Seno Mexicano. Martín Salinas, an authority on the pre-Columbian peoples of the area, estimated that at least half of the Indians lived in the Río Grande delta region, where there were abundant food resources.

In the southernmost part of the region lived the culturally advanced *Huastecos*, who were the heirs of the *Olmec* civilization, the oldest in Mesoamerica. But these inhabitants proved to be the exception in the Seno Mexicano, where the natives dwelled in very primitive conditions. To the west, in the Sierra Madre Oriental, there came to live refugee peoples who had fled from the northward-advancing Spanish frontier. Also present, by the mid-1500s, were *Tlaxcalan* peoples from the region near Mexico City. In return for their alliance with Cortés in defeating the Aztecs, Tlaxcalans were granted privileges by the Spanish, which included opportunities to colonize the northern regions. They also took part in Spanish explorations of the Seno Mexicano.

Hostile Indians raided Spanish settlements along the western boundary of the Seno Mexicano for over 150 years, effectively halting the advance of colonization. Finally, spurred by the looming threat of a foreign presence on the Gulf coast, as well as by the continued Indian menace, the Spanish colonized the Seno Mexicano in the middle 1700s.

As the Spanish-speaking newcomers came into the coastal region, they encountered its principal native culture. Known collectively as "Coahuiltecans" or *Coahuiltecos*, these peoples roamed the area of present-day Tamaulipas and southern Texas. According to border historian Jerry D. Thompson, the Coahuiltecans included several subgroups: *Katuhanno, Bobole, Pachal, Kesale-Terkodams, Payayas, Aranamas, Tamiques, Oregons, Carrizo*, and the cannibalistic *Karankawas* along the middle Texas coast. In addition, there were other small bands, to whom Spanish chroniclers ascribed names because their original identities were unknown. For instance, in the Mier and Roma area lived the *Garzas, Zalayas* and *Malahuecos*. The *Tareguanos, Pajaritos, Paysanos, Venados, Cueros Quemados* and *Guajolotes* inhabited the Camargo and Rio Grande City district. Finally, the *Comecrudes, Tejones y Sacatiles, Pintos, Nazas* and *Narices* lived in the vicinity of Reynosa.

Both Spanish accounts and present-day scholars describe the lifestyle of the Seno Mexicano natives as nomadic. There is evidence that, at times, some of the Indians planted crops, but most essential to their survival was the hunting of deer, antelope, rabbits, rodents, reptiles and birds. Along the coast, Indians supplemented their diet with fish. Their only domesticated animal, according to Spanish accounts, was the dog.

A major portion of the diet for the Coahuiltecans was vegetarian, including *pitayas* (a cactus berry), *maguacata* (ebony tree fruit), *mesquitamal* (mesquite bean), *panal de miel* (wild honey), *nopalitos* (prickly pear), *pichilinge* (a red berry from the cactus plant) and *chágüite* (hard gum from the bark of the mesquite). Many of these foods are still consumed today by Mexican Americans in South Texas.

Peyote was a popular drink of the Coahuiltecans. While a strong hallucinogenic, it was not habit-forming, and was used for its medical and tonic qualities, as well as for religious ceremonies. Essential to the Indians' well-being were medicinal herbs, such as *yerba anís*, for calming frightened persons; *estafiate, muicle, cuajil, yerba buena* and *manzanilla*, to cure indigestion; *yerba del zape*, to remove warts; *cenizo*, to relieve colds; *mejorana*, to diagnose colic; and *amargoso*, to reduce fever. Today, these cures still serve the local *curanderos* (folk healers) well.

Warfare among the Coahuiltecans consisted of hit-and-run tactics. Common sources of conflict ranged from fighting over women to securing better hunting grounds. The victors frequently crowned their success with the taking of scalps and captives whom they ate during their victory celebrations. This cannibalistic practice also included their own fallen warriors.

Cannibalism, according to Spanish accounts, was common among the Karankawas. Alvar Núñez Cabeza de Vaca, who may have traveled through the area in the 1530s, also reported the practice of female infanticide among the Indians along the Río Grande. He claimed this was done to prevent daughters from falling into the hands of their foes, thereby increasing the number of their enemies.

In describing the lifestyle of the natives, the Spanish chroniclers had a vested interest. The more primitive the natives could be depicted, the greater the perceived need and justification to colonize their lands and Christianize them. This rationale is very much in evidence in the remarks of Juan Rodríguez de Albuerne, Marquís de Altamira, and a member of the commission charged with approving colonization plans for the Seno Mexicano. According to Rodríguez, the Indians

> *. . . live without religion, without fixed habitation, without dress, who, like wild and wandering beasts, occupy the coast of the Mexican Gulf, its ports, its famous salines, rich rivers, healthful plains, fertile lands and valuable minerals. With their murders, thefts, fires and all kinds of inhuman tactics, they desolate entire jurisdictions, provinces, cities, villages and Christian settlements along the southern, western and northern confines of their haunts. They obstruct roads, paralyze commerce and occasion incalculable losses to the royal treasury daily with the increased annual costs involved in the maintenance of presidios and the organization of campaigns.*

This official left no doubts about the urgent need to convert and colonize these native people. It was a justification that Hernán Cortés and many other Spaniards utilized time and again to expand Spain's empire in the New World. The rationale differed little from that of other European powers who colonized the western hemisphere.

Although there is much evidence, both written and archaeological, which tells about Coahuiltecan life, there still remains an untold version of this story—namely, the Coahuiltecan one. Unfortunately, the Indians had no written language, and were unable to record their side. Otherwise, we could undoubtedly read about their anxiety and fear of unwelcome foreigners whose arrival threatened their property, lifestyle and very lives.

Despite the unflattering accounts about the Coahuiltecans, their legacy is a vital part of the region's heritage. Their vegetarian diets and medical cures have already been noted. In addition, their racial assimilation with the colonizers contributed to the growth of the mestizo people in Mexico. Indian contacts with the Spanish were frequently violent. Yet there were also some definite benefits derived from the meeting of these peoples. In short, it was the beginning of that blending of cultures that has shaped lower Río Grande history—a shared experience between the Spaniards and the Indians in the Seno Mexicano.

Early Spanish Explorers in the Seno Mexicano

Prior to the conquest of the Aztec empire by Hernán Cortés and his Indian allies (1519-1521), there were several Spanish voyages of exploration into the western gulf of Mexico. For example, Francisco Hernández de Córdova probed the coastal waters of the Yucatán and Vera Cruz in 1517, and the next year, a small fleet under Juan de Grijalva y Cuéllar followed in de Córdova's wake, sailing perhaps as far north as the Río Pánuco. Neither of these ventures resulted in any attempts at settlement.

In 1519, probably after hearing of de Córdova's and Grijalva's discoveroes, the governor of Jamaica, Francisco de Garay, sent Alonzo Alvarez de Pineda with four ships to explore the Gulf of Mexico's coastline. Garay hoped that Pineda would find an all-water route to the Orient, which would bring great riches and prestige to the governor. Pineda followed the coast from today's Florida westward to Texas (making him, probably, the first European to see that land) and, finally, northeastern Mexico. After an unfriendly encounter with Cortes' men near Vera Cruz—the Conqueror wanted no intruders in "his" Mexico—Pineda withdrew northward to the Río Pánuco and established Garay's Colony. He may have returned, then, to Jamaica; but Garay apparently sent him back quickly with supplies for the fledgling colony.

Garay sent supplies in 1520, in a fleet commanded by Diego de Camargo. He delivered his cargoes, but soon afterward the Huastec natives, angered by Spanish mistreatment, destroyed the colony and captured all but two ships. Among the dead was Pineda. Camargo and other survivors struggled to reach Vera Cruz; Camargo died of wounds, but others made it and joined Cortés. Meanwhile, Garay, hearing nothing more from his colony, determined to go himself. With eleven ships he sailed in 1523, arriving at the river he named the *Río de las Palmas*, north of the Río Pánuco. For a long time, it was popularly believed that this river was today's Río Grande. But, most likely, it was the *Río Soto la Marina*, about 150 miles south of Matamoros. Finding the surrounding country "worthless" and almost uninhabited, Garay went south to the Pánuco, by then under Cortés' control. The governor of Jamaica died while a "guest" of Cortés, his efforts to colonize the Gulf coast a failure.

The next Spaniards arrived in the Seno Mexicano more by accident than design. In 1528, Pánfilo de Narváez headed an expedition from Cuba to the west coast of Florida. From there, part of the expedition sailed westward along the Gulf coast and became shipwrecked—probably on present-day Galveston Island, where Cabeza de Vaca and his three companions were captured and enslaved by the Karankawas. Finally, some six years later, the four survivors escaped and fled south to the Río Grande, which they apparently crossed somewhere between Brownsville and Laredo. From there they traveled northwest to the El Paso region, where Cabeza de Vaca heard about the "Seven Golden Cities of Cíbola." Their wanderings ended at Culiacán in western Mexico, where they found other Spaniards. De Vaca's accounts of fabulous wealth and golden cities sparked the expedition of Francisco Vásquez de Coronado (1540-1542) into the present-day southwestern United States. But Cabeza de Vaca brought no news of riches in the Seno Mexicano; as a result, that territory remained unattractive for settlement for two centuries.

The only area of the Seno Mexicano that actually attracted a settlement prior to the 18th century was in the southeastern corner. Since the 1530s, Franciscan missionaries had begun an evangelization program among the Indians along the Río Pánuco. One of the missionaries, Fray Andrés de Olmos, moved to the north bank of the river and founded the Villa de San Luís de Tampico in 1560. A less savory excursion was made in the 1580s by conquistador Luís de Carvajal, who rounded up Indians for slave labor in the mines of Nuevo León, of which he was governor.

Fray Juan Bautista Molinedo, a Dominican missionary in the early 1600s, founded Indian missions at Tula and Palmillas in the southwestern district of the Seno Mexicano. Constantly harassed by Indian raids and without government protection, the missionary reluctantly abandoned his efforts to convert the natives.

The long, desolate coastline of the Seno Mexicano made it vulnerable to intrusion by foreign powers. By the 1560s, French and English ships were sailing boldly into the western Gulf, which the Spanish viewed as "their sea." The unwelcome intruders raided Spanish towns and made off with loot. In the years that followed, periodic reports of foreign ships and explorers reached Mexico City, alarming the viceroyalty and prompting expeditions to find and destroy the invaders. A force under Jacinto de Sepulveda crossed the Río Grande in the 1630s, to search for strange white men with "red legs"—probably Dutch seafarers—reported on the coast by Indians. In the most famous such episode, the explorer LaSalle founded his French settlement on the middle Gulf coast, north of Corpus Christi Bay, in 1685. Indians told Spanish frontier officials in Nuevo León of the French presence on the coast and even on the Río Grande (La Salle himself may have probed as far as present-day Laredo), and Spanish forces began hunting for the intruders. In two expeditions, Alonzo de León searched the lower Río Grande on its south and north banks, but could not find the Frenchmen. Meanwhile, LaSalle's ill-fated colony had failed, its leader shot and his men either killed by Indians or forced to flee to Louisiana. In 1689, de León's son and namesake found the ruins of LaSalle's Fort St. Louis near Matagorda Bay. Together, these foreign incursions made it imperative that Spain initiate firm steps to colonize the territory.

Compounding the fear of foreign aggressions were the frequent Indian raids on Spanish settlements along the western border of the Seno Mexicano. Along with the need to terminate those Indian raids came the pleas of missionaries to evangelize the natives. Thus, many powerful incentives converged to prompt the colonization of the Seno Mexicano.

Escandón's Colonization Plan

During the opening decades of the 18th century, the colonization of the Seno Mexicano became a high priority for the Spanish government. On July 10, 1739, King Philip V issued a *cédula* (order) creating a *junta* (commission) to examine colonization proposals and to recommend a leader to carry out the project. By the time the junta convened, three colonization proposals awaited review, all of which the commission found too costly. Likewise, the junta found the applicants unqualified for the task. It was not until 1746 that a new candidate appeared on the scene—*Don* José de Escandón, whose credits included successful pacification of Indians in the Querétaro area, as well as excellent administrative skills. Especially pleasing to the commission was his frugal colonization plan.

Born on May 19, 1700, in the province of Santander in northern Spain, Escandón joined the military at the age of 15. Shortly thereafter, his military duties took him to Mérida, Yucatán, where he served until 1721. His next assignment transferred him to the militia in Querétaro, where he commanded units engaged in subduing Indian uprisings.

Escandón's military successes and humane treatment of native captives earned him much praise and promotion in rank. Collectively, these military experiences qualified him to undertake the colonization of the Seno Mexicano.

Besides being a skilled military leader, Escandón demonstrated success in business ventures, which included a textile enterprise and cattle ranching. These operations made him prosperous and provided ready capital to invest in colonization projects. In short, the crown officials saw in Escandón an able administrator, a frontier diplomat who knew how to deal with the Indians, and a prosperous merchant. The last of these traits was of special interest to the crown, for it preferred private wealth to finance colonization.

In September of 1746, Escandón received authorization from the king that he was to head the colonization of the Seno Mexicano. Before a trial colonization project could be implemented, Escandón needed to conduct exploratory expeditions, called *entradas,* to gather information on the native inhabitants, geography and natural resources. Escandón had already consulted a number of reports from entradas made in previous centuries, but he planned to make a seven-point entry into the Seno Mexicano to provide him with much more detailed and precise information about the area. Furthermore, his plan was both cost effective and timesaving.

On January 24, 1747, Escandón began the first entrada with 150 men. Starting in Querétaro, he traveled northeastward across the Sierra Madre Oriental and arrived at Soto la Marina. Along the route, he reported seeing land suitable for agriculture, and good fishing. From Soto la Marina, he headed northward to the mouth of the Río Grande. When he arrived at Río Conchas (currently named San Fernando) on February 10, he discovered valuable *salinas*, or salt deposits. Here, Escandón met another entrada coming from Linares in Nuevo León under the command of Antonio Ladrón de Guevara with 53 soldiers. Before meeting the Linares entrada, Escandón had planned to meet an expeditionary group coming from the south. The southern one had started as two separate groups, one from Tampico under the leadership of Francisco de Sosa with 175 men, and the other from Villa de Valles, led by Juan Francisco de Berverena with 200 men. The two groups converged in the Sierra de Tamaulipas, a lateral range of the Sierra Madre Oriental, and from there, the Villa de Valles party continued its trip northward to the Río Grande. Inclement weather hindered the group's travel, causing them to miss their appointment with Escandón at the Soto la Marina area. Consequently, they continued their trip alone to the Río Grande.

On the final leg of the journey to the Río Grande, Escandón encountered hostile Indians, whom he appeased with gifts. He halted the expedition at the mouth of the river on February 24th, 30 days after he had started in Querétaro. Here he waited for the arrival of three other expeditions— one of 42 men, under the leadership of Blas María de la Garza Falcón from Cerralvo in Coahuila, who traveled along the south side of the Río Grande toward its mouth; the second, a group of 50 men under the command of Miguel de la Garza Falcón from Monclova, also in Coahuila, that crossed the Río Grande above Laredo and explored the northern side of the river to its mouth; and finally, the last expedition, a group from La Bahía del Espíritu Santo composed of 50 soldiers led by Captain Joaquín de Orobio Bazterra, that trekked southward to present-day Raymondville, and from there, westward to complete their journey near present-day Roma. The task of exploring both sides of the river between Roma and its mouth fell upon the Cerralvo and Monclova parties. Arriving shortly after Escandón at the mouth of the river, the Cerralvo and Monclova parties arrived and reported that, despite stretches of barren land, the area was suitable for raising cattle and sheep. The La Bahía commander's report was more promising in that along the gulf coast, he had encountered land highly suitable for agriculture and ranching. Generally, he found the Indians to be friendly but primitive—except for the Karankawas, who he claimed resisted all efforts to convert them to peaceful co-existence.

After returning to his headquarters at Querétaro, Escandón completed his report to the Crown on October 26th, 1747. He recommended the establishment of 14 settlements—two on the Texas coast, and the other 12 in present-day Tamaulipas. He also recommended that these settlements be located where adequate natural resources were available and where there would be natural protection against native uprisings. To attract settlers, he proposed offering land, subsidies and ten years of tax exemptions, which he felt should first be offered to the participants in the entradas. He did not believe that presidios were necessary because the settlers could defend their own land. Finally, he encouraged the establishment of Indian missions under the supervision of Franciscans, who he said could also serve the spiritual needs of the Spanish settlers. The report first went to the viceroy in Mexico City, and from there to the king, who gave his approval on October 23, 1748. Along with the approval, the king granted Escandón the title of Conde de la Sierra Gorda and made him a Knight of Santiago, the most distinguished military order in Spain.

Colonization of the Seno Mexicano

On June 1, 1748, Escandón received word from the viceroy to start preparations for colonizing the Seno Mexicano. He immediately advertised his colonization project in the neighboring provinces, where he hoped to attract the needed number of settlers in addition to those who had accompanied him on the *entradas* of 1747. He promised free land, tax exemptions for 10 years and money to defray moving costs. At the same time, he realized that the original request from the royal treasury for 58,000 pesos was inadequate, and requested that the crown increase the amount to 90,000 pesos. By December of 1748, all was ready to begin colonization.

The colonization of the Seno Mexicano took some six years, and became the largest such undertaking in the western hemisphere. Since it was such an extensive project, this account will focus only on some of the major settlements, and especially on those along the Río Grande. Escandón left Querétaro in December of 1748 with 750 soldiers and more than 2,500 settlers. After crossing the Sierra Madre Oriental into the Seno Mexicano, he planted the first *villa*, the settlement of Santa María de Llera, south of present-day Ciudad Victoria. He placed Captain José de Esajadillo in charge of 11 soldiers and 44 families. After founding the villa, Escandón established others, including Santander, present-day Jiménez, on February 17, 1749, which he placed under the command of Captain Antonio Ladrón de Guevara. The settlement started with some 60 families and subsequently became the seat of government for the new province of Nuevo Santander, which Escandón named after his home province on the northern coast of Spain.

Next he dispatched two of his captains to establish villas, while he pushed northward to the Río Grande where it met the Río San Juan. It was here that some 40 settlers from the neighboring province of Nuevo León, under the leadership of Captain Blas María de la Garza Falcón, had established Villa de Nuestra Señora de Santa Ana de Camargo on March 5th. When Escandón arrived a few days later, he ordered the building of a house for priests and an Indian mission, called San Agustín de Laredo. He placed Fray Marquís in charge of the mission. Marquís later became the superior of all Franciscan missions in the province of Nuevo Santander.

At almost the same time as the founding of Camargo, Captain Carlos Cantú established a settlement about 30 miles down the river with 40 families from Nuevo León. Escandón, who arrived at the site on March 14th, named it Reynosa, and selected a site for the Indian mission of San Joaquín del Monte.

During this time, in 1749, the province's northern boundary was not firmly set. Instead, it was a vaguely-defined area along the Río San Antonio and the Río de las Nueces. Escandón attempted to place settlements on both rivers, to help anchor the northern end of Nuevo Santander; but neither effort was successful, due to a lack of settlers and unfavorable conditions for settlement.

After these failures, Escandón turned his attention south of the Río Grande, to inspect the progress of previous settlements and to found new ones. By the end of the spring of 1749, the colonizer had established 13 villas. At this time, Escandón realized that it would be necessary to begin more settlements than had originally been planned in order to secure communication routes. After a brief inspection of his province, he founded the Villa de Santa María de Aguayo on October 3, 1750, which, after Mexico's independence, became Ciudad Victoria. The villa, with some 24 families under the direction of Captain Juan Antigárraza, had a nearby Indian mission.

While the governor was occupied with settlements in the southern half of his province, ranchers from the provinces of Nuevo León and Coahuila traveled to the Río Salado, where it empties into the Río Grande, about 20 miles up the river from Camargo. There, 64 families under the leadership of Nicolás de la Garza, Antonio Taveres and Vicente Guerra received approval from Escandón on October 10, 1750, to found the settlement of Revilla. Also established was the nearby Indian mission named Ampuero.

Across the river, 26 miles to the northwest of Revilla, a Coahuilan rancher by the name of José Vásquez Borrego began a ranch settlement with 13 families. Escandón approved that settlement on August 22, 1750, and named it Nuestra Señora de los Dolores. The settlement never became a villa and had no Indian mission. The ranchers remained dependent on the missionary in Revilla for their spiritual needs.

Midway between Camargo and Revilla, on the Mexican side of the Río Grande across from present-day Roma, another group of ranchers started a settlement. The key leaders in this venture were Prudencio Orobis y Bazterra, Blas María de la Garza Falcón, José Florencio de Chapa and Manuel de Hinojosa. In the beginning, the settlement of 19 families was part of the jurisdiction of Camargo, but in 1752 it achieved separate status and was named Mier. These ranchers, like those on Borrego's ranch settlement, depended upon Revilla for spiritual sustenance.

While Escandón was visiting Revilla in 1754, he received word that Captain Tomás Sánchez of Coahuila wanted to start a villa on the north bank of the Río Grande, to be named San Agustín de Laredo. The governor first wanted the settlement further north on the Río Nueces, but the captain convinced him that the location was unsuitable for settlement. At the time of its official founding on May 15th, 1755, Laredo had about five families. Located in semi-arid terrain, it developed into a ranching community with very little farming. For its spiritual ministries, it had to depend on Revilla.

By the fall of 1755, Escandón had completed his colonization work. In his report of October 13th, he described the many hardships the early settlers faced, but despite these difficulties, the settlements were on their way to becoming self-sufficient. He reported the founding of 23 settlements, consisting of 1,481 families—6,383 settlers. To this number he added 2,837 mission Indians. The 23 settlements were almost double the number that he had originally planned. The governor was convinced that, for all practical purposes, the colonization of his province was finished and the only royal financial support needed was for the Indian mission.

In the report, Escandón reminded the Spanish authorities that all land had been granted in common. He thought that common holdings during the early years of a settlement's existence would assure town development and avoid the disputes which might have occurred with individual land grants. In the case of the latter, he advised making these grants at a later date, when there was time to develop criteria for awarding private land grants. In addition to common land grants already mentioned, the governor had granted common lands to support the Indian missions.

Testimony for Escandón's successful colonization can be found in the José Tienda de Cuervo report. After the governor submitted his report in 1755, Viceroy Agustín de Ahumada y Vallalón, in accordance with Spanish policy, ordered an inspection, or *visita*, of the Province of Nuevo Santander. He appointed José Tienda de Cuervo and Agustín Lopez de la Cámara Alta to carry out the visita, which they completed by October 13, 1757, and submitted their report to the viceroy in Mexico City.

The commissioners reported that an additional villa had been started in 1755, bringing the total number of settlements to 24, with nearly 9,000 inhabitants. The ranching statistics showed 58,000 horses, 25,000 cattle, 1,874 burros and 288,000 sheep and goats. The largest number of sheep and goat ranches were in the jurisdictions of Camargo, Revilla and Mier. Ranching was the principal source of wealth in the province, while agriculture, consisting of beans, maize and vegetables, was supplementary. The commissioners pointed approvingly to the increasing importance of trade in salt, fish, beef, veal, mutton, hides and tallow. A section of the report was devoted to the spiritual development of the province, which noted 22 Franciscan missionaries ministering to some 1,400 Spanish families and several hundred Indians.

The official inspectors offered a number of recommendations: the reduction of military forces, and concentration of remaining soldiers in the southern and western regions of the province, where they were most needed; the division of common lands into individual land grants, so as to increase agricultural and livestock production; and finally, the establishment of several more settlements. The tone of the report left no doubt that the inspectors were satisfied with Escandón's work.

Escandón's administration of his province very much suited the governing ideals of the Bourbon rulers of the Spanish Empire. These rulers wanted efficiency, minimum costs and economic productivity. The governor could also point to his successful pacification and Christianization of the native inhabitants. Furthermore, his administrative skills were very much in evidence in his selection of well qualified leaders to carry out settlement projects. Equally important was his promotion of a diversified economy and a road system to further trade and communication in the province. In fact, the basic road system in Tamaulipas today still follows the routes established by the governor of Nuevo Santander.

Ten years later, in 1767, there was a second visita in the province. This one was ordered by the then Viceroy Carlos Francisco de Croix, who placed Juan Fernando de Palacio in charge of the visita. The purpose of this inspection was to examine the progress of the province since 1757 and to implement the division of common land holdings into individual grants. In making the division, Palacio designated three types of land holdings—land that could be irrigated, grazing land and town land. The major criteria for determining individual grants were based on the number of years of civilian and military service and the number of years a settler had lived in a villa or settlement.

In keeping with centuries old traditions that the Spaniards had inherited from the Romans, the royal surveyors laid out town plots in grid form, starting in the center with the plaza, which was reserved for the church, municipal building and jail. Adjacent to the town were lands called *ejído,* to be used by town residents to grow crops and raise livestock for daily needs. Beyond the ejído, the surveyors plotted *porciones* which along the river measured 9/13 of a mile wide and then extended 8 to 16 miles away from the river. This type of land grant assured the owner of access to water. Beyond the porciones were larger grants, mostly suitable for grazing.

Taking formal possession of land required much ritual, which started with a Mass. After this, each prospective grantee went to the property, where the new owner and a priest performed a ritual designating ownership. The act concluded with the signing of official documents of ownership that were deposited in government archives.

After the royal surveyors had completed their task of surveying villas and land grants, they marked out the mission lands. Here they merely confirmed mission grants that had already been designated by Escandón. In the case of Mier, a settlement that had no mission, the surveyors set aside land and designated it for an Indian mission.

The Palacio visit again confirmed Escandón's successes. It was welcome news in the final years of his life. Plagued by illness and allegations of misuse of public money, he had been forced to relinquish his governing duties. He was eventually cleared of the allegations, but was unable to enjoy the victory, for the court decision did not come until three years after his death.

Despite these misfortunes at the end of his life, Escandón left a legacy that became the dominant way of life along the lower Río Grande for over 150 years—namely, ranching and the unique lifestyle that developed along with it. His settlers pioneered the livestock industry that became the North American cattle trade of the 19th century.

Nuevo Santander & Mexican Independence

The closing decades of the colonial era witnessed few changes in the daily lives of the citizens of the province of Nuevo Santander. Ranching, with limited agriculture, continued to be the order of the day. Nuevo Santander ranchers found ready markets for their livestock and byproducts at various fairs throughout the Kingdom of New Spain. Although somewhat isolated by the Sierra Madre Oriental from the rest of New Spain, Nuevo Santander was not immune to major developments beyond its borders. This was the case with the insurrection of Padre Miguel Hidalgo y Costilla against the Spanish government in Mexico City in 1810, which ultimately led to the independence of Mexico in 1821. For the province of Nuevo Santander, the insurrection had long range consequences.

The *Grito* (cry or shout) *de Dolores* by Father Hidalgo on September 16, 1810, called for an end to colonial rule in New Spain, but professed loyalty to King Ferdinand VII. Essentially, the grito was a call for more local autonomy. The rebellion began in Hidalgo's parish town of Dolores and spread throughout the Guanajuato region and south into the present-day state of Michoacán. Eastward, Hidalgo's army marched to the outskirts of Mexico City. At the same time, the parish priest of Dolores sent Padre José María Morelos south into Guerrero to gain control of the region south of Mexico City. After leaving the Valley of Mexico, the rebel army marched to Guadalajara where, on the outskirts of the city, they were soundly defeated on January 17, 1811, by a well-disciplined Spanish army under the command of General Félix Calleja. Hidalgo and a small remnant of his army were able to escape and flee northward to Saltillo, which was then under the control of rebel forces. After leaving the city, Hidalgo and his followers hoped to find refuge in Texas and, if necessary, in the U.S. Unfortunately for the rebels, a small Spanish force ambushed them north of Saltillo at the wells of Baján on March 21st. After a brief trial, all the rebel leaders were executed within a few months. The same fate awaited Morelos four years later.

Throughout the brief period of the Hidalgo rebellion, there were only ripple effects in Nuevo Santander, mostly in terms of Spanish troop movements and destruction of property by rebels. Two leading supporters of the Hidalgo movement were José Bernardo Gutiérrez de Lara and his brother Padre José Antonio, descendants of the founders of Revilla. The padre devoted his efforts to propagandizing for the Hidalgo cause, and his brother served in the insurgent army. After Hidalgo's defeat in 1811, José Bernardo fled to the U.S. as an emissary for the insurgents to seek help from President James Madison. Later, he went to Louisiana, where with Augustus William Magee, he led an expedition into Texas. They captured San Antonio and declared independence from Spain on April 6, 1813, but the independence was short-lived. The following August, royalists managed to end the insurrection at the Battle of the Medina, south of San Antonio. José Bernardo again fled to the U.S., where he remained until the successful conclusion of Mexican independence.

In the closing years of the colonial era, Nuevo Santander became the scene of another rebellion against Spain. In 1817, Xavier Mina, an exiled Spanish liberal, landed with a small force near Soto la Marina, with the hope of joining forces with survivors of the Hidalgo insurrection. The ill-fated expedition quickly ended with the capture and execution of Mina by Spanish authorities. It was not until four years later that Nuevo Santander, like the rest of Mexico, peacefully gained independence from Spain under the *Plan de Iguala* of Agustín de Iturbide. With the acceptance of the Plan, Nuevo Santander became a province in Iturbide's empire.

The imperial rule of Iturbide ended abruptly in 1823, when republican factions forced Iturbide's resignation and adopted the federalist Constitution of 1824. Under the federalist structure, many of the old colonial provinces were converted into states. Nuevo Santander, now renamed Tamaulipas, retained its old colonial boundaries, which with its northern boundary of the Río Nueces, became a bone of contention between the U.S. and Mexico. The provincial headquarters was changed from Santander to Aguayo, now renamed Ciudad Victoria after the president of Mexico, Guadalupe Victoria. The change of fortunes enabled José Bernardo Gutiérrez de Lara to return from exile in the U.S. and become the first governor of Tamaulipas.

Tamaulipas and Texas Independence

The arrival of the 19th century witnessed a significant development in the Tamaulipas economy. In 1796 a group of settlers founded Congregación del Refugio, later renamed Matamoros, near the mouth of the Río Grande. By the end of the 1820s, the port city had become an important international trade center with close to 300 foreign residents. Many of these foreigners, as well as the Mexican merchants, supplied goods to major fairs in Mexico, especially to those in Monterrey and Saltillo.

Among the foreign merchants were Francis Stillman from Connecticut and Henry Austin, a cousin of Stephen F. Austin. The latter, in 1829, attempted to start a steamboat line up the Río Grande to Revilla, but this venture was not successful. Further evidence of the rapidly growing commercial center was the more than doubling of the city's population from 1829 to 1837 (7,000 to 16,372). Despite the years of turmoil in central Mexico and the Texas independence movement, the city merchants, according to Armando C. Alonzo in his *Tejano Legacy*, were very resilient and manged to recover after these setbacks. The export-import trade of Matamoros added a new dimension to the ranching economy of Tamaulipas and helped to fulfill the dream of Escandón, who in his colonization plans desired a diversified economy.

As in previous times, external affairs ended up having the greatest impact on the new state. The assumption of the Mexican presidency by Antonio López de Santa Anna in 1833 resulted in the demise of both federalism and the Constitution of 1824. The president's return to centralism and dictatorial rule aroused opposition among republican factions, who demanded the reinstatement of the Constitution of 1824. Throughout Mexico, there were rebellions against Santa Anna and separatist movements in the states of Zacatecas and Yucatán. The most serious of these rebellions developed in Texas, where *tejanos* and newly-arrived Anglo-Americans agitated for the restoration of the Constitution. The revolt came to a head when the Texas rebels succeeded in driving General Martín Perfecto de Cós, the brother-in-law of Santa Anna, out of San Antonio in December of 1835. Tamaulipas did not remain immune to these external events, which had both immediate and long-range consequence for the state.

In responding to the capture of San Antonio by the Texan rebels, Santa Anna marched an army of 6,000 across the Río Grande near Laredo in February 1836. On his right flank, the president ordered General José Urrea, stationed in Matamoros with 1,000 men, to move north to Goliad and prevent any attack from the east, while Santa Anna laid siege to San Antonio. The strategy proved successful. In a costly victory, the rebel garrison in the Alamo fell to the Mexican forces on March 6, 1836. A second rebel army, captured at Goliad, was executed under Santa Anna's orders; only a few Texans escaped. There still remained Sam Houston's army east of San Antonio, which Santa Anna pursued. Houston's retreat ended with the Battle of San Jacinto on April 21st, when the outnumbered Texans fell upon Santa Anna's army encamped near present-day Houston. The extent of the Mexican defeat became all too evident when General Urrea returned to Matamoros with survivors of the battle numbering only some 3,000—less than half of the original invading forces.

The capture of Santa Anna, and his signing of the Treaty of Velasco on May 14, 1836, had long-range repercussions for Tamaulipas. The treaty called for Mexican recognition of the independence of the Republic of Texas, with the Río Grande as its southern boundary, rather than the traditional boundary of the Río Nueces. Later, the Mexican congress refused to recognize the independence of the new republic and rejected the treaty. Texas, in a state of shambles and confusion, was in no position to enforce its boundary claim. Neither could Mexico, shaken by internal dissent and power struggles. The result was continued "brush fire" conflicts between the two republics, eventually culminating in the annexation of Texas by the U.S. and a war between the U.S. and Mexico. With these developments, the inhabitants of Tamaulipas were no longer on the periphery. This time, they, and especially the people of the lower Río Grande region, became eyewitnesses and participants.

Tamaulipas and the Mexican-American War

Shortly after the independence of Texas, Tamaulipas itself became the scene of a separatist movement. On November 5, 1838, Antonio Canales, a former Tamaulipas state legislator, issued a proclamation supporting federalism at Guerrero, formerly known as Revilla. With the help of Antonio Zapata from the same town, Canales gained control of Mier, Matamoros and Soto la Marina. Even Monterrey and Saltillo briefly fell into federalist hands. After intermittent fighting in 1839, Canales called for the establishment of the Republic of the Río Grande on January 1, 1840 and elected Jesús Cárdenas from Reynosa as president. The new republic included the states of Nuevo León, Coahuila and Tamaulipas. In very short order, Mexican troops, under the command of General Mariano Arista, defeated the separatist movement near Saltillo on October 23, 1840—a defeat that ended the life of the Republic of the Río Grande after a mere 283 days.

With the defeat of federalism in Tamaulipas, the Mexican government again turned its attention to Texas, whose sovereignty it never recognized. In February 1842, General Rafael Vásquez led an army of 400 into Texas, occupied San Antonio for a few days, and then withdrew. At the same time, other Mexican troops briefly occupied Goliad and Refugio. A much larger Mexican force under General Adrián Woll, briefly took San Antonio again in September of the same year. Retaliating for these Mexican incursions, General Alexander Somervell, Secretary of War for the Republic of Texas, led an undisciplined force of Texan volunteers to the Río Grande in 1842. After much pillaging and plundering along the river, a mutiny developed after which William S. Fisher took command. The Texan government ordered the expedition's recall. But Fisher, determined to inflict vengeance on the Mexicans, led some 260 men, along the north bank of the river and crossed over to take Mier. There, he met a much larger Mexican force of 600 under the command of General Pedro de Ampudia and suffered defeat with 248 of his men taken prisoner. The fact that Mexican troops, on two occasions, briefly occupied San Antonio and other towns, and the fact that Texan retaliations were unsuccessful, made it clear that the Republic of Texas was unable to defend its sovereignty. The setbacks served as convenient arguments for those who wished to be annexed to the U.S. to assure protection against foreign threats, especially from Mexico.

The Texan supporters of annexation to the U.S. found a powerful ally in "Manifest Destiny," a popular and growing view among many Americans that their brash, young republic was destined by Providence to extend to the Pacific coast, taking in all other lands along the way. Manifest Destiny embodied the country's expansionist views and became an important plank in James K. Polk's presidential campaign platform of 1844 which supported annexation of Texas. He won the election, held on December 4th. The day before, lame-duck President John Tyler had called on Congress to annex Texas. Soon after, Mexico broke off diplomatic relations with Washington, for it believed Texas to be sovereign Mexican territory. The march to war between the two republics had begun.

But diplomatic concerns over possible Texas annexation were not the only ingredient in the brewing storm in Washington. Slavery, and the growing rift between South and North over it, was the real problem. Texas—settled densely by Southerners—would be a Southern, slave-holding state. Abolitionists saw Texas as a major threat to their power in Washington and to their cause. A South increasingly dependent upon the cotton-plantation system for its economic and political strength viewed Texas as essential—not only as a slave state rich in cotton production, but also as a potential year-round land route linking a possible Southern confederacy with the far Southwest and Pacific Ocean trade. Northerners saw the same potential for Southern strength, and the "Texas question" became the focus of heated, angry debates in Washington and across the country. For all sides—North and South, Americans and Mexicans, tejanos and "Texians"—the stakes in Texas were enormous, and the outcome of the contest would determine the future of two nations. Early in 1845, James Polk played his hand, and a deadly game ensued along the lower Río Grande.

When Polk took office in March of 1845, he recognized the old Texan claim to the Río Grande as the southern boundary. He then ordered General Zachary Taylor and an American army to Texas to safeguard American interests against "foreign" incursions. Mexico, incensed, began mobilizing her military forces. The long drum roll leading to war had begun. For a year, Taylor's army camped at Corpus Christi, on the south side of the Nueces River—land viewed by Mexico as its own. In December, 1845, the United States formally annexed Texas. In the Spring of 1846, Polk ordered Taylor to march to the Río Grande to enforce the new international boundary claim. The Americans arrived opposite Matamoros on March 28th. General Pedro de Ampudia ordered the invaders to withdraw north of the Nueces. Taylor refused and began building an earthen fort. Both sides sent out mounted patrols. A clash was inevitable, and it happened in April, at Rancho Carricitos upriver. Mexican cavalry surprised and defeated a U.S. patrol, causing casualties on both sides. Word was sent to Washington, and Polk had his war. In May, he addressed the Congress, stating that "American blood had been shed upon American soil," and called for a declaration of war. Despite opposition from abolitionists and others, there was enough enthusiastic support to carry the measure. (As the war went on, casualty lists grew, and opposition to it also grew. Among those calling for an end to it by 1847, was an Illinois congressman named Abraham Lincoln, who pointedly asked to know the exact spot on which American blood had been shed.)

By the time Congress declared war on Mexico, the first two battles had been fought, both near present-day Brownsville. General Mariano Arista led a 6,000-man force across the Río Grande and clashed with Taylor's forces at Palo Alto on May 8th. Outnumbered some 3 to 1, Taylor's men used their superior training, leadership and artillery to defeat Arista. The next day, the Americans won an even more decisive battle in the tangled thickets of Resaca de la Palma, forcing Arista to retreat across the river and abandon Matamoros. Ten days later, Taylor occupied that city. Then, without opposition, he moved upriver to occupy Reynosa and Camargo, securing both sides of the Río Grande.

Taylor continued to build up his invasion force that summer, and advanced toward Monterrey. He took the city in a 4-day battle in September. His successes made him the best-known American soldier and a prime presidential candidate for the Whig Party (predecessor to the Republican Party). To derail this political threat, Polk and his Democratic cabinet ordered General Winfield Scott (himself eyeing the White House) to appropriate most of Taylor's veteran troops for his own planned invasion of southern Mexico at Vera Cruz. Despite the loss of his veteran troops, Taylor and his remaining forces met and turned back a Mexican army under Santa Anna, at La Angostura, near Saltillo in early 1847, known in U.S. history as the Battle of Buena Vista. Scott, meanwhile, occupied Vera Cruz and marched overland to Mexico City. The outnumbered *norteamericanos* defeated the larger enemy forces along the way. In American eyes, the fault lay not with the bravery of the Mexican soldiers, (of whom the U. S. troops often spoke highly, but with the training and leadership abilities of the Mexican officer corps which the *yanquis* considered inferior. Scott went on to occupy the Mexican capital in October of 1847.

Hostilities officially ended with the Treaty of Guadalupe-Hidalgo on February 2, 1848, in which Mexico ceded about one half of its territory to the United States. Those regions, which stretched between the Great Plains and the Pacific, became today's western and southwestern states, from Colorado to California, and from Wyoming to New Mexico and Arizona. The Treaty established the Río Grande as the boundary line, and required the U.S. to pay a $15,000,000 indemnity to Mexico, along with the recognition of Spanish and Mexican land grant titles in territories surrendered to the U.S. Unfortunately, there was no provision giving specifics as to the process for validating the titles.

With the Río Grande replacing the Río Nueces as the northern boundary of Tamaulipas, it became more a case of the border crossing the people than the people crossing the border. The change of boundaries opened the way to migrations from the U.S. into the South Texas triangle, where like the original settlers, newcomers engaged in ranching and other commercial ventures. It was a continuation of the shared experience that had been characteristic of the region since the days of the Seno Mexicano.

The Shadow of Statehood over the Río Grande Valley

In delineating the Río Grande as an international boundary, the Treaty of Guadalupe Hidalgo confirmed the existence of the region of South Texas. Even before the national authorities had ratified the Treaty, government leaders in Austin moved aggressively to extend its jurisdiction to the lower Río Grande.

As a strategy to block the possibility of a federal solution to the land problem in the region, the legislature in 1848 hastily created three counties along the Río Grande. Beginning at Laredo in the north, with the formation of Webb County (in memory of James Webb, former secretary of state in the Republic of Texas), the line of rural government extended down to Starr (as a tribute to Dr. James Harper Starr, land agent, banker, and Treasurer of the Republic of Texas), and Cameron (in honor of Captain Ewen Cameron, a member of the disastrous Mier Expedition into Mexico in 1842). Subsequent sessions of the state legislature strengthened the line of county government along the Río Grande.

In 1850, the Congress of the United States took up the sweeping issue of the disposition of territory recently acquired from Mexico. Several proposals, including the creation of the Territory of New Mexico and compensation to the State of Texas for the loss of its northwestern land claims, occupied the attention of Congress. In anticipation of a final solution to the land issue, on February 2, 1850, a group of newcomers in Brownsville, mostly lawyers, merchants, ranchers, and steamboat captains, augmented by a cadre of Hispanic proprietors, convened in a rural schoolhouse to draft petitions to Congress. Convinced that state government was insensitive to their special interests, and proud of the material culture they had built in the form of warehouses, wharfs, and a robust trade with Mexico, the organizers of the meeting (Elisha Basse, Sam A. Belden, R. H. Hord, F. J. Parker, Joseph Z. Palmer, and Stephen Powers) persuaded their supporters to adopt a two-part proposal recommending to Congress the separation of the Trans-Nueces watershed from the rest of Texas by creating a Territory of the Río Grande.

The separatists dispatched the first petition to Senator William H. Seward of New York, and the second to Senator Henry Clay of Kentucky. Unfortunately the timing of these solicitations cluttered, rather than clarified, the debates in Congress, particularly the issue of delineating the boundary between a reduced State of Texas and an emerging Territory of New Mexico. Senator Clay, one of the renowned architects of the Compromise of 1850, scuttled the proposal submitted by the Brownsville separatists.

The publicized goals of the separatists galvanized a vocal opposition from the conservative element in Brownsville society, represented by Judge Israel Bonaparte Bigelow. As a jurist who instinctively understood the complexity of land issues in an isolated border environment, Bigelow successfully campaigned for the office of state senator, a post he held from 1851 to 1853. Aware of an urgent need to establish another unit of rural government to administer the Spanish and Mexican land grants, and particularly the old *porciones* formerly monitored by the *Ayuntamiento* of Reynosa, Senator Bigelow introduced a bill to organize Hidalgo County, located between Cameron and Starr and named in honor of Padre Miguel Hidalgo, instigator of the movement for Mexican Independence. Although Bigelow had established a lucrative practice litigating land titles, and in spite of the fact that he periodically invested in real estate ventures, the senator, unlike the separatists, proclaimed faith in the ability of state government to dispense justice in South Texas.

Piqued by the criticism of the Brownsville separatists, the Texas Legislature adopted a measure authorizing the appointment of a special commission to authenticate claims of all Spanish and Mexican land grants in the Trans-Nueces region. Governor Peter H. Bell in 1850 assured the residents of the Río Grande counties that the appointment of William H. Bourland and James R. Miller to head an investigative commission would not disturb legal titles and would actually promote stability and prosperity along the border.

In the process of examining land claims throughout the Valley, the commissioners compiled an extensive collection of documents, including survey field notes, verifying the legitimacy of many grants. To continue their work below Río Grande City, the commissioners transferred their base of operations. Carefully packing the documents into a wooden crate, they boarded the river steamer *Anson* for a short trip to their next destination. Unfortunately the steamer sank, destroying tons of cargo and the crate of invaluable records!

To offset the disaster, the Bourland-Miller Commission submitted a lengthy list of land titles to the Texas Legislature for confirmation. The legislators approved an "Act of Confirmation" and instructed the General Land Office to issue certificates to owners of the approved land grants. Regrettably, in compiling the original list, the commission scribes omitted many names of land holders, an oversight that spawned unending litigation.

Notwithstanding the passion of county politics, the litigious nature of the land claimants, and the prosperity of some border merchants, the Valley receded into isolation from the rest of Texas. Surrounded by sparsely populated, semi-arid regions, the border area maintained a tenuous connection to San Antonio and other towns in Central Texas by a few narrow wagon roads. The railroads beginning to radiate out of Galveston and Houston virtually ignored South Texas, forcing travelers and merchants of the region to depend mainly on wagon trains and riverboats for transportation.

The Pre-Civil War Experience

In the decade following the end of the Mexican-U.S. War, the heavy influx of Anglo Americans into the Trans-Nueces region contributed another layer of shared experience to the Rio Grande Valley. The

U.S. Army established its presence at Fort Brown in Brownsville, Ringgold Barracks at Rio Grande City, and farther north at Fort McIntosh in Laredo. Supplying the military installations became an important priority of the War Department. Distributing supplies from the San Antonio depot via overland routes always remained an option, but eventually steamboats on the Río Grande became a faster medium of delivery to riverside docks. Charles Stillman, a Connecticut Yankee, became involved in the profitable steamboat trade, along with Mifflin Kenedy, a skipper from Pennsylvania, and Richard King, of New York and a veteran of the Indian wars. Kenedy and King formed a partnership, M. Kenedy & Company, with Stillman as a silent partner. Soon, with a flotilla of twenty-six steamboats, they dominated the post-war commerce on the Río Grande. Remaining in business from 1850 to 1874, King, Kenedy, and Stillman amassed respectable fortunes which they later invested in ranch lands in South Texas.

Before the Civil War, Brownsville developed into the principal Texas community on the lower Río Grande. In addition to the resident tejanos whose ancestry stretched back to the Escandón era, the population, numbering more than 500, included artisans, boatmen, soldiers-of-fortune, Eastern speculators, and hundreds of land-hungry immigrants (mainly English, French, German, and Irish). A few African Americans of non-slave status melded with the pedestrians who daily tromped the dusty streets. Operators of barber-shops, bordellos, hardware stores, livery stables, pool halls, restaurants, and saloons actively competed for the trade of the town's fluctuating population. By 1850, Israel B. Bigelow, heading a movement to establish municipal government, volunteered to serve as Brownsville's first mayor. The city council, controlled by Anglo American aldermen, enacted ordinances to regulate the commercial, residential, recreational, and social life of the community. With pride, the council pointed to the vitality of trade at the town market and to the inaugural edition of *The Rio Grande Sentinel*, Brownsville's first regular newspaper.

Charles Stillman arrived in Matamoros in 1828 to establish a mercantile business. In partnership with José Morell, he also opened retailing outlets in Brownsville, including one of the first textile factories, and later branched out into silver mining in Mexico. After the Mexican War, during which his venture with King and Kenedy flourished, Stillman diversified his business portfolio to embrace the real estate next to Fort Brown. He sold city lots, many of which fronted on the Río Grande, and named the townsite Brownsville. In honor of his wife, who preferred not to dwell in Texas, Stillman named one of the principal streets Elizabeth.

Stillman's contemporaries in the business life of Brownsville included Francisco Yturria, a Basque immigrant who converted an inheritance of a tailor shop in Matamoros into a prosperous mercantile enterprise. Through frugal investments in land and commerce, Yturria became a wealthy and influential pillar of border society. Another Basque immigrant, José San Román, likewise established a thriving mercantile business that enabled him to contribute to the development of South Texas.

Alberto Campione, an immigrant from northern Italy, traveled the coastal road from Brownsville to Port Isabel. Anglicizing his name to Albert Champion, the Italian built a lucrative business in merchandising, ranching, and farming. As his wealth mounted, Champion persuaded three of his brothers to emigrate to Texas.

Another newcomer to the Valley, Stephen Powers, a Yankee lawyer with prior service as American consul in Switzerland and a brief tour as legal aide to General Taylor, endured the hardships of border living while he waited for favorable opportunities. After the war, Powers reaped the benefits associated with service as county and district judge, customs collector, mayor, state representative, and state senator.

The façade of tranquility in South Texas politics and business shattered in 1859. Juan Nepomuceno Cortina, a self-styled *caudillo* and avenger of injustices perpetrated against Mexican Texans by an alien legal system, led a daring raid in Brownsville to rescue a *vaquero* who worked at his mother's Rancho del Carmen.

Cortina was not a stranger in the Valley. Born in 1824 in Camargo, Cortina enjoyed the material benefits as a member of a land-wealthy family. His mother's vast estate extended to the north bank of the Rio Grande that included much of the terrain surrounding present-day Brownsville. However, despite Cortina's belief that he had the right to inherit his mother's "Brownsville" lands, he ultimately, through a variety of legal wranglings, lost them to Charles Stillman, who subsequently developed the properties as part of the Brownsville townsite.

At the outset of the U.S.-Mexican War in 1846, Cortina, a member of an irregular cavalry unit, participated with General Mariano Arista's forces at the battles of Palo Alto and Resaca de la Palma. After the war a Cameron County grand jury indicted Cortina on charges of cattle rustling, but he never stood trial because of his skillful ability to blend into the cultural landscape to avoid arrest.

Cortina remained an irritant to law-enforcement officials in the Valley, including companies of Texas Rangers and the U.S. Army. In the autumn of 1859, after committing a second raid against the Brownsville jail, Cortina withdrew into the wilderness. Merchants on both sides of the river clamored for military action to restore law and order. Late in the year a combined militia from Brownsville and Matamoros, called The Tigers, took the field against the caudillo, believed to be ensconced at Rancho del Carmen. Cortina's followers easily defeated The Tigers, capturing much of their artillery and munitions.

Although humiliated, the Brownsville group retaliated after the arrival of a company of Texas Rangers, led by Captain William Tobin. To demonstrate their resolve, a citizens group pressured the county sheriff to hang Tomás Cabrera, one of Cortina's men captured earlier in the year by a local posse. Cortina capitalized upon this gruesome incident to rally the support of Spanish-speaking residents of the lower Valley with inflammatory proclamations. After the hanging he asked Governor Sam Houston to defend the human and property rights of Mexicans and Mexican Americans in Texas.

Ultimately, a coalition of commercial and political interests on both sides of the border defeated Cortina. During the American Civil War, he aided the Union forces in the Valley. At the same time, during the French Intervention in Mexico, Cortina fought courageously in the nationalist forces of President Benito Juárez. In the turmoil following the collapse of Maximilian's Empire, Cortina proclaimed himself governor of Tamaulipas, but soon relinquished the office to a higher-ranking general. A successor president of Mexico, Porfirio Díaz, who favored commercial development and the creation of a modern infrastructure, disapproved of Cortina's unpredictable behavior which threatened the fragile stability of the border. The president invited the loyal general to Mexico City, gave him a sinecure and a comfortable residence, and effectively removed him from the border. Cortina died in a suburb of Mexico City in 1894, at the age of seventy.

The Civil War In South Texas

Secession and Civil War, events that originated far away on the Atlantic side of the continent, soon engulfed the inhabitants of South Texas. On January 28, 1861, delegates at the Texas Secessionist Convention voted to remove Texas from the Federal Union. Presented to the public in a state-wide referendum, the Ordinance of Secession garnered the approval of the voters 46,129 to 14,697.

In the borderland, the decisive vote in support of secession to the contrary, the outcome reflected more the vested interests of regional *políticos* who wished to align themselves with the Confederate apparatus in Austin than to a commitment to defend slavery and the states' rights ideology. In the line of communities from Brownsville to Laredo, the census rolls of 1860 identified only fourteen slaves, the chattels of Anglo professionals or merchants, almost all of whom were either females or children (seven in Cameron County, six in Starr County, and one in Hidalgo County).

At the outbreak of the Civil War, even before the days of a compulsory draft, an exceedingly vexing situation of divided loyalties arose among the Spanish-speaking population along the Río Grande, from Zapata to Cameron counties. Unionist sympathizers in the region cleverly exploited perceived cracks in Confederate defenses.

In some respects the Civil War in South Texas evolved as a continuing saga of the Cortina controversy. Two days before the surrender of Fort Sumter, South Carolina, on April 12, 1861, Antonio Ochoa launched a revolt against Confederate authorities in Zapata County. Advancing toward the county seat of Carrizo (renamed "Zapata" in the 1890s), Ochoa's partisans, numbering about forty, not only threatened to hang Sheriff Pedro Díaz, but vowed to prevent officials from taking an oath of allegiance to the Confederacy. County Judge Isidro Vela confronted Ochoa's motley crowd and persuaded them to return to their homes. As they retreated downriver, the dissidents proclaimed their defiance of the Confederacy and its supporters.

Meanwhile, Confederate Captain Matthew Nolan, former sheriff of Nueces County, promptly assembled a relief company of twenty-two soldiers to assist the officials in Carrizo. With the arrival of Nolan's Confederate troupe, Judge Vela issued warrants for the arrest of Ochoa and his band of dissidents. Captain Nolan, accompanied by Judge Vela and Sheriff Díaz, led his small company south of Carrizo to Rancho Clareño, which Pedro Ochoa used a headquarters.

The Confederates reached the ranch before dawn on April 15. As Nolan deployed his troops around the perimeter of the ranch, the sheriff called upon Ochoa's pro-Unionists to surrender. Some insurgents started to comply with the order, but one of them commenced firing upon the Confederates. Nolan then ordered his troops to attack the insurgents. In the assault, the Confederates killed nine of Ochoa's followers, some of whom were unarmed. Although Ochoa escaped unharmed across the river, two of his chief lieutenants died in the battle.

The incident at Rancho Clareño solidified the Hispanic resistance in Zapata County which loosely meshed with the Cortina conflict on both sides of the border. Some Tejanos fled across the river to avoid Confederate harassment, only to discover later that their lands had been confiscated, based on a legal interpretation spawned by the Texas Revolution that sanctioned the practice of dispossessing refugees, especially those of another culture, of their possessions for allegedly abandoning their ownership or aiding the enemy. From the Confederate perspective, the presence of a disloyal Mexican Texan element made it imperative for the military to divert a complement of troops from Ringgold Barracks to the town of Carrizo to protect the lives and properties of steadfast Confederates.

Confederate officers, anxious to win glory in combat and rapid promotions, viewed an assignment to South Texas as unpopular border guard duty. Enlisted personnel, recruited in the more populated humid regions of Texas, likewise preferred garrison duty elsewhere. At Fort Brown the situation closely approximated the perplexity in Zapata County.

Apart from the danger of military hostilities, the Civil War opened business opportunities to individuals willing to take risks in the pursuit of profit. Brownsville became a gateway to Matamoros and the nearby port of Brazos Santiago. Under these circumstances, the best arrangement Confederate officers could negotiate with Mexican authorities in Matamoros was the declaration of a neutral zone. Attracted by Mexico's shield of neutrality, scores of speculators and suppliers, normally unattached Anglo adventurers, flocked into the lower Valley. Typifying the rush of speculators, George Washington Brackenridge amassed a fortune trading with Yankee ship captains, much of which he dispensed later as philanthropic gifts throughout the state.

The Civil War battles in Texas, generally minor engagements confined to peripheral areas, spared the state of deep-seated, lingering animosities that plagued the South beyond the period of Reconstruction. Compared to fierce engagements that occured east of the Mississippi River, the Texas battles commemorated in local folklore lacked the significance of major turning points in the Civil War. Nonetheless, the occurrence and outcome of such battles affected the lives and fortunes of people who dwelled in the vicinity.

Of the numerous engagements that occurred along the length of the Río Grande from Laredo to Boca Chica Pass, three achieved memorable importance. By the summer of 1863, the tide of the Civil War started to shift in favor of the Union forces. Exiled Unionists from Texas recommended to President Lincoln a Federal occupation of the Río Grande. The architects of the Union plan were Edmund Jackson Davis, an attorney and district judge before the Texas secession, Leonard Pierce, Jr., American consul in Matamoros, and John L. Haynes, a Mexican War veteran and politician who chose to live in Rio Grande City. Besides choking the flow of Southern cotton into Mexico, which would wreck the Confederate economy, the Unionists believed a Federal presence in South Texas would send unequivocal signals to Emperor Maximilian that the United States of America strongly disapproved of the violation of Mexican sovereignty.

On November 2, 1863, a Union force of nearly seven thousand troops, commanded by General Nathaniel Prentiss Banks, disembarked at Brazos Island and hoisted the American banner. In Brownsville, Confederate General Hamilton Prioleau Bee, with fewer than a hundred soldiers to defend the city, panicked. To salvage as much as possible, he dispatched a long wagon train conveying valuable provisions to safety near the Río Nueces. Next, he ordered his soldiers to transport cotton bales, stockpiled in warehouses, across the river to Matamoros. Furthermore, he ordered the troops to destroy the inventory that could not be moved, either by burning or dumping the bales into the river. Finally, on orders from the general, the Confederate troops set fire to Fort Brown. Out of control, the flames spread to adjacent buildings along the waterfront. Adding to the chaos and public horror, the arsenal at Fort Brown, containing eight thousand pounds of gunpowder, exploded, casting a shower of sparks that ignited more fires. In the confusion, General Bee evacuated all remaining Confederates from Brownsville.

Four days after the fire that destroyed an entire block of buildings and damaged other properties, General Banks led the initial contingent of the Union Army, the Ninety-fourth Illinois Volunteers, into Brownsville along Elizabeth Street. Later, the First Missouri Light Artillery and the Thirteenth Maine Volunteers marched into the city to reinforce the Federal presence in South Texas.

A few weeks later, Union Colonel Edmund J. Davis, in command of the First Texas Union Cavalry, a contingent of more than thirteen hundred troopers, proceeded upriver to seize Ringgold Barracks at Rio Grande City. Colonel Santos Benavides, C.S.A., with a small force withdrew from the garrison and forded the river. Remaining in the lower Valley to recruit another cavalry unit, Colonel Davis sent a vanguard of two hundred Federals to reconnoiter the retreating Confederates.

Davis and Haynes, assisted by Consul Pierce in Matamoros, recruited volunteers for a Second Texas Cavalry, composed primarily of Spanish-speaking residents of both sides of the river. Adrián J. Vidal, stepson of Mifflin Kenedy and a former Confederate captain, volunteered for service in the Union cavalry. The Second Texas Cavalry, commanded by Colonel Haynes, performed mostly scouting missions to the Río Nueces and north along the Río Grande. On March 19, 1864, Davis, with two hundred troops of the Union First Texas Cavalry, confidently advanced upon Laredo. With limited resources and ample determination, Colonel Santos Benavides and a guard of forty veteran fighters, repulsed the Union cavalry. Greatly humiliated, Colonel Davis withdrew to the lower Valley.

Late in the war, in San Antonio, Confederate Colonel John Salmon "Rip" Ford recruited volunteers for a new unit he stylishly called the "Cavalry of the West." In the summer of 1864 he proceeded into South Texas. On July 30, 1864, Ford's fighting cavalry expelled the Union forces from Brownsville. The following spring, Colonel Ford fought the last land battle of the Civil War at Palmito Hill east of Brownsville. On May 13, 1865, the Confederate cavalry defeated a sizeable force of 800 Union troops en route to Brownsville. From the Union prisoners the Texas victors learned that the Confederate government had fallen a week earlier and that the war was over. Sorrowfully, in surrendering their swords the Confederate victors became the vanquished in South Texas.

Vicissitudes of Reconstruction

Reconstruction in Texas officially commenced from a wharf in Galveston on June 19, 1865, when Brevet General Gordon Granger proclaimed the emancipation of the slaves. Assuming command of all forces in Texas, the general declared that Union troops would be assigned to interior posts and to the Río Grande. In the border counties, besides enforcing the terms of the surrender and preserving order until a civil government could be established, army personnel received directives to conduct a demonstration of strength against the French in Mexico.

The French adventure exacerbated the instability of life on the south bank of the Río Grande. In compliance with a diplomatic accord to compel the Mexican government to make payments on foreign loans, French armed forces, together with contigents of British and Spanish troops, invaded Veracruz late in 1861. Torn apart by years of internal strife, Mexico had defaulted on its payments to the foreign bankers who appealed to their respective governments to collect the debt through military intervention. As France's imperialistic goals in Mexico became apparent, Spain and England withdrew from the tripartite adventure.

Left alone in Mexico, France increased the level of its armed forces with which it imposed a foreign emperor, Maximilian, a member of the Hapsburg dynasty of Austria. In addition to French regulars and Belgian auxiliaries, the imperialists recruited native Mexicans to augment their military presence. From strongholds in northern Mexico, the nationalist forces under Benito Juárez waged guerilla warfare against the imperialists. By late 1864, the two sides were locked in a struggle to control the lower Río Grande.

In September, 1864, as the American Civil War trundled toward its end, pro-French General Tomás Mejía, backed by a small flotilla of gunboats and steamers, seized control of Matamoros and much of Tamaulipas. Mejía's presence in the region incited tension on the north bank of the river, as scores of survivor refugees, caught in guerrilla skirmishes between French imperialists and juarista nationalists, flocked into South Texas. The news of General Lee's surrender at Appomattox, at first cheered because the fighting had ended, turned into anxiety about what an imminent Reconstruction might entail. Throughout the remainder of 1865, sporadic warfare between imperialists and juaristas contributed to the instability. Finally, in June 1866, in the hills of Santa Gertrudis, near the town of Camargo, juarista forces, commanded by General Mariano Escobedo, decisively defeated the French imperial army and foretold the termination of the second Mexican Empire. A year later, with the capture and execution of Emperor Maximilian and General Mejía at Querétaro, the empire permanently collapsed.

Following the ascent of General Porfirio Díaz to the presidency of Mexico, for the first time border officials along the south bank of the river endeavored to eradicate lawless elements from their midst. Juan Nepomuceno Cortina, quite elegant in an army general's uniform, received orders to report to Mexico City for consultation. Virtually controlled by the creature comforts Don Porfirio bestowed upon him, Cortina never returned to the border. Another general, Ramón Treviño, governor of Nuevo León, typified the emerging change in public policy in Porfirian Mexico of making the roads safe for travelers and merchants.

On the Texas side of the river, the U.S. Army enhanced its presence with the deployment of additional personnel, and with the disbursement of equipment, arms, munitions, and construction materials, to Fort Brown, Ringgold Barracks, and Fort McIntosh. For border security, the military extended its line of garrisons to Fort Clark (Bracketville) and Fort Duncan (Eagle Pass).

To test the safety of the border, merchants from San Antonio traveled in heavy wagons loaded with trade goods. Crossing at Laredo-Nuevo Laredo, they continued their journey to Monterrey and Saltillo. Most affluent travelers, however, preferred the relative convenience of Concord stagecoaches. The stage line ran from San Antonio to Eagle Pass, then across to Piedras Negras, and then to Monterrey. Notwithstanding these modes of modern transportation, the main flow of traffic to Porfirian Mexico advanced along the northern edge of the region. South Texas, military security to the contrary, remained practically isolated during the last quarter of the nineteenth century.

Advent of the Railroad

The lower Rio Grande Valley leaped into the twentieth century in 1903, when developers and promoters announced the coming of a railroad. Actually, the concept for a railroad originated with Colonel Uriah Lott, of Albany, New York, who arrived in Brownsville in 1867. Impressed with the topographical possibilities but in need of gainful employment, he migrated north to Corpus Christi. By 1871, as owner of a commission house, he chartered sailing vessels to transport hides and wool to New York buyers. Later, as director of the Corpus Navigation Company, Lott endeavored to improve the channel and wharf facilities. Then he turned his attention to railroad development. Essentially a promoter and not a financier, the colonel enlisted the backing of Mifflin Kenedy and Richard King in constructing the Corpus Christi, San Diego, and Rio Grande, a narrow-gauge railroad that, completed in seven years, ran from the coast to Laredo.

In 1884, Colonel Lott relocated in Bexar County to promote the construction of the San Antonio and Aransas Pass Railway. Constantly looking for new horizons, Lott convinced Benjamin Franklin

Yoakum, traffic manager of the S.A.A.P. Railway, to investigate the possibility of tapping the agricultural and pastoral resources of the lower Rio Grande Valley. Preoccupied with other priorities, Yoakum waited until the beginning of the twentieth century before sending Captain J. E. Hinckley to reconnoiter potential routes for a railroad through the Valley into Mexico.

Lott's earlier successes, combined with Yoakum's surveys, attracted prestigious endorsements on both sides of the border. President Theodore Roosevelt, who advocated an inter-ocean canal through the Isthmus of Panamá, and President Porfirio Díaz, who welcomed foreign investors into Mexico, encouraged Yoakum to pursue his objective. Prominent investors in South Texas (Robert Driscoll, Sr., John G. Kenedy, Caesar Kleberg, Robert J. Kleberg, and John J. Welder) rallied behind the project. On January 12, 1903, upon receiving a charter from the State of Texas, the directors elected Colonel Uriah Lott president of the St. Louis, Brownsville, and Mexico Railway. Shortly afterwards, construction crews arrived in the Valley to create the necessary infrastructure. First, they built a steel bridge over the Río Grande, between Brownsville and Matamoros, to accommodate locomotives, wagons, and buggies. Next, they planned the routes to connect South Texas with geographically distant terminals in San Antonio, New Orleans, Chicago, and Memphis.

The town council of Brownsville voted incentives to keep the promoters committed to the enterprise: a bonus of 12,000 acres of land on either side of track, not to exceed a distance of four miles, $40,000 in cash, an urban tract of forty to fifty acres to support a depot, and an additional twenty acres for maintenance shops and storage sheds. The bulk of the financing came from St. Louis, Missouri. Lon C. Hill, reportedly the most influential citizen for a quarter-century, organized a group of railroad boosters to generate widespread support for the project in South Texas. Rentfro B. Creager, statewide leader of the Republican Party, served as secretary of Hill's booster club. Thirteen members with Spanish surnames represented a third of the membership.

Appropriately, on July 4, 1904, the first train of the St. Louis, Brownsville, and Mexico Railway rolled into the southern terminal at Brownsville. In the meantime, reassured that the railroad had become a reality, Yankee speculators and their Texas workers founded three towns along the projected line of track at the northern edge of the region: Robstown (for Robert Driscoll, Corpus Christi banker, lawyer, and land speculator), Bishop (in honor of F. Z. Bishop, a Corpus Christi insurance agent and land developer), and Kingsville (initially a tent city for construction workers). At the southern end, other towns rapidly proliferated along the right-of-way and commemorated aspects of the Valley heritage: Raymondville (in honor of Captain E. B. Raymond, manager of *El Sauz*, a component of the King Ranch), Harlingen (in honor of the ancestral home in the Netherlands of Uriah Lott, friend of Lon C. Hill and the moving force behind railroad construction in the Valley), La Feria (a Spanish land grant), Mercedes (Spanish for "land grants," chosen from suggestions sent to the St. Louis, Missouri office of the Rio Grande Land & Irrigation Co., owners of the townsite property), Weslaco (acronym for W. E. Stewart Land Company), Donna (for Donna Fletcher, postmistress), Alamo (Spanish for Cottonwood; the town of Ebenezer, when transferred to a source of sweet water surrounded by cottonwood trees, assumed the name suggested by the ecology), San Juan (for John Closner, developer of San Juan Townsite Co. and owner of San Juan Sugar Plantation), Pharr (Henry N. Pharr, sugarcane grower from Louisiana), and McAllen.

The work of John McAllen signified an effort to shift some of the economic-political influence from

Brownsville toward the interior of the Valley. McAllen arrived in Brownsville shortly after the Mexican-American War and found employment as a clerk in a store operated by John Young, husband of Salomé Ballí, a land-wealthy heiress whose holdings extended for miles along the north bank of the Río Grande into neighboring Hidalgo County. In 1859, when John Young died, the widow owned property in excess of $125,000. By virtue of the decedent's will, John McAllen became manager of the estate. Two years later, McAllen married the widow Salomé and initiated a concerted plan to enlarge the Ballí properties with additional land purchases in Hidalgo County. Eventually, the prosperous McAllen ranch became a beacon to attract the railroad into the interior.

The advent of the railroad, together with the introduction of surface irrigation, transformed the Valley into an elongated band of potential cultivation of agricultural and citrus products. Land values adjacent to the road bed jumped upward. Coincidental with the arrival of the railroad, an acre of land sold for fifty dollars in 1906. Four years later the valuation increased to three hundred dollars per acre. Demographic patterns in the Valley changed, as streams of migrating farmers from the mid-west and refugees escaping the violence of the modern Mexican Revolution converged in South Texas.

In 1900, the population of Cameron County barely topped 16,000; thirty years later the statistics exceeded 77,000. Hidalgo County's population jumped dramatically from 6,534 in 1900 to 38,110 in 1920. A decade later, Hidalgo caught up with Cameron County in population density, signifying the effectiveness of John McAllen's plan to share the benefits of the political-economic base of the region. By 1930, the aggregate population of the four Río Grande counties surged upward to 176,000.

John McAllen succeeded in creating a power shift from Brownsville to Hidalgo County. Likewise, he attained another goal of enticing the railroad to construct a spur line into his ranch property near the river, naming the end-of-tract after himself. He failed, however, in his quest to designate his townsite as the county seat. In fact, the choice of a site for the county courthouse precipitated a power struggle among several communities. Initially, La Habitación, a rustic town less than a mile from the border, served as the first county seat. In 1852, John Young, a native of Scotland and a recent immigrant in the Valley, persuaded officials to change the name of the county seat to Edinburgh, reminiscent of Edinburgh, the Scottish capital. Later, in 1876, the name was changed to Hidalgo. In 1908, after the arrival of the railroad, Hidalgo County partisans of John Closner, eager to thwart the ambitions of municipal leaders in Mercedes and McAllen, succeeded in transferring the courthouse to their own townsite of Chapin, a small, centrally-located community with a railroad spur line. Named originally for D. B. Chapin, prominent lawyer and County Judge, the town was renamed Edinburg in 1911, after its namesake was involved in a controversial San Antonio shooting. (Chapin was cleared of any wrong-doing, and remained a figure in Hidalgo County law for many more years.) In reviving the old name of the first county seat on the river, the "h" was dropped from the end.

The Legacy of the Twentieth Century

In penetrating the lower Río Grande country, the railroad contributed to the phenomenon of the shared experience. However, the successful entry of the railroad also invited competition: within a few years the Texas legislature appropriated funds to construct public highways connecting the Valley with other parts of Texas and the nation. As the burgeoning "automobile age" spread across the country, the railroads began feeling its effects. Just before World War I, a diminishing volume of traffic forced the St. Louis, Brownsville & Mexico Railway into bankruptcy, leading to its later absorption by the Missouri Pacific system. After the war, Valley agriculture expanded as American consumers demanded more of its products. In the revitalized economy, the railroad enjoyed renewed prosperity in the Valley, while confronting the competition from commercial trucking.

The early 1900s again brought violence to the borderlands. In Mexico, decades of mounting discontent under Porfirio Díaz' absolute rule finally erupted in 1910. The Mexican Revolution tore that country apart, and set various military/political leaders—Madero, Huerta, Carranza, Villa, Zapata, and others—against one another in a years-long struggle. Engulfing northern Mexico, the fighting inevitably came to the border. Sporadic raids into the Valley by mounted revolutionaries came closer to all-out guerilla war in 1915, following the disclosure of the *Plan de San Diego*—an anarchist scheme to foment racial violence against Anglo-Americans through an armed uprising by minorities in the American Southwest. Drawn up by several anarchists from South Texas and northeastern Mexico, the planned bloody revolt never occurred, but the revealing of it set border nerves on edge, and sent shock waves to Austin and Washington, D.C. A cycle of attacks and retaliations gripped the lower Río Grande, as Texas Rangers and, later, great numbers of National Guard troops from many states were sent in to quell the revolutionaries' raiding. The soldiers also had another mission—to act as the spearhead of invasion, should the U.S. and Mexico again go to war.

But the threat of war with Carranza's Mexico in 1916 diminished, to be replaced by the real war of 1917. With the U.S. entry into World War I, most border troops were withdrawn for service in France. A military presence along the boundary remained, however, as unrest in Mexico continued. By 1920 the "Great War" was over and the Mexican Revolution was winding down. For the next 20 years, the Army's border forces were small, until war clouds gathered again. In the meantime, the Valley region enjoyed prosperous growth in its widespread farms and the towns and small cities which served them. Prohibition meant little, with Mexico's *cantinas* just across the river, and even the Great Depression's full impact was not felt for some time.

Just before the outbreak of World War II, the Rio Grande Valley manifested a combination of urban growth and rural serenity. Intensified agriculture produced an amalgamation of farms, orchards, stores, processing plants, allied industries, and distribution centers. Besides the renowned citrus products (oranges and grapefruit), the Valley exported a variety of vegetables (beets, cabbage, carrots, corn, green beans, onions, potatoes, and tomatoes). In the postwar period, cotton and sorghum emerged as important export crops.

The face of the region had changed, just as it had so many times before. From a desolate area inhabited by native peoples, to a Spanish colony defined by its ranching traditions, to a booming agricultural mecca, the lower Río Grande witnessed many transformations. Even now, its metamorphosis continues, as industry and international commerce take center stage. But at its core, this region is about the blending of cultures and perspectives—each wave of newcomers making its new stitch in the ever-changing tapestry. The story of the lower Río Grande is best told within the context of this remarkable diversity—a shared experience that will continue to define it for centuries to come.

*Cited in Paul Horgan, *Great River: The Rio Grande in North American History* (New York, Chicago and San Francisco: Holt, Rinehart and Winston, 1954), 341-342.

THE

JOSÉ CISNEROS

COLLECTION

Paleo-Indian Hunters—c. 8000 BC

The earliest known culture in the New World is called Paleo-Indian, or "ancient Indian," by anthropologists. Brought by those who first migrated across the Bering Strait from Asia millennia ago, Paleo-Indian culture and life evidently centered on hunting the many game animals which roamed the Americas. In time, Paleo-Indians spread throughout both continents—including the region of today's southern Texas and northeastern Mexico.

Some 10,000 years ago, herds of mammoth and mastodon, camels, horses, giant bison and other Pleistocene fauna wandered this area, as evidenced by fossil remains. No doubt, many such animals were stalked by Paleo-Indian inhabitants, armed with razor-sharp flint weapons; rocks and other handy projectiles were most likely used as well.

Paleo-Indians were skilled hunters and consummate users of tools that they fashioned from materials in their environment. This region must have been especially demanding, with its rugged landscape of flood plains and plateaus and scant natural resources, although there may have been more water holes and springs than today. Their main weapon was the stone-tipped dart. Hurled with a throwing stick, or *atlatl*, it could penetrate the toughest bison or mammoth hide at close range. Clothing made from animal skins and sandals of woven plant fibers probably helped to protect the wearers from the elements.

Little of Paleo-Indian material culture remains. Most has long since been consumed by the moisture-laden soil and the climate. But their tell-tale weapon points—such as Clovis, Folsom, and Angostura types—have survived and serve as mute reminders of the long-ago dawn of early human life in this rugged land.

Northern Mexico Salt Traders at Sal del Rey Lake—c. 1400

Salt. A humble commodity, yet essential to life. Salt lakes, or *salinas*, known and valued since prehistoric times, are found along the lower Río Grande. The best known of these is *El Sal del Rey*, in northern Hidalgo County. Further east, lies *La Sal Vieja*. The region's native peoples obtained salt from such places, for their own use and, evidently, for trade. So valuable was the white mineral, that cultures far to the south knew about these Río Grande salinas, and according to Spanish accounts, often sent trading parties to the region.

For many decades there have been traditional stories that even the Aztec empire tapped El Sal del Rey for salt. Behind such stories often lies a core of truth, and archaeology has turned up evidence of trade between this region and its neighbors —particularly the Huastecan peoples of the Mexican Gulf Coast, from Tampico down to Vera Cruz. Huastec pottery vessels found near Brownsville and obsidian points traceable to outcrops deep in the Mexican interior indicate that the peoples of the Río Grande had something worth trading. While the region's highly developed shell-working industry doubtless played a role—elaborate shell jewelry occurs in local burials, and was probably a desired item in trade—the chief lure may well have been salt. It is not hard to imagine a trading party at El Sal del Rey, a supervisor watching as workers filled baskets with salt to be carried back to the south by human "pack trains." Some haggling over the rate of exchange probably took place, perhaps in sign language.

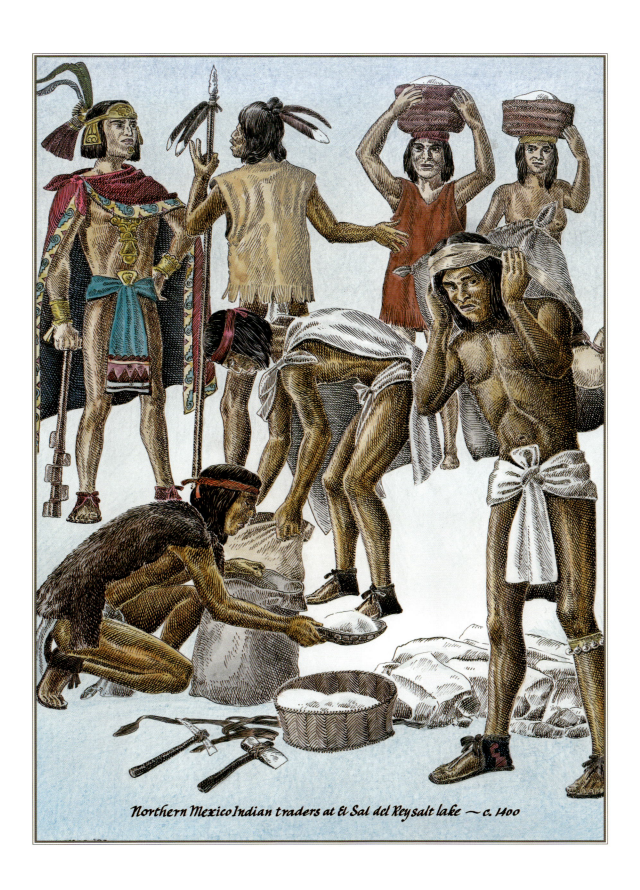

Northern Mexico Indian traders at El Sal del Rey salt lake — c. 1400

Coahuiltecan Indian—c. 1500

When Spaniards first came to the lower Río Grande in the 1500s, they found Native American peoples who lived mainly by gathering edible plants and hunting game. Anthropologists now call them *Coahuiltecans**, after their language group, characteristic of Indians in the state of Coahuila. But these many small tribes had their own names and their own distinct culture, which the Spanish *padres* saw little reason to note. While a fair knowledge of Coahuiltecan life and ways has been gleaned from Spanish accounts, most of the record is silent. By 1800, warfare, disease and assimilation into the Spanish/Mexican population had reduced the native peoples greatly. Within another 80 years they were all but gone, and their centuries-old culture a vanishing memory.

Coahuiltecans inhabited much of present-day South Texas and Tamaulipas. Those dwelling along the Río Grande and other streams enjoyed, perhaps, a greater abundance of food and resources than others, whose existence was among the most primitive in North America. Theirs was a mobile way of life—one of seasonal migrations within established territories, taking advantage of food resources at each new location. Material culture was reduced to essentials—baskets, gourds, bone and antler tools—which were easily carried. Clothing, except in winter, was sparse or absent. Little is known about their diet, society, religion or medicine, except for tantalizing fragments in Spanish writings—and in the journal of Cabeza de Vaca, the shipwrecked castaway whose wanderings through the region gave him a first-hand familiarity with its native peoples; his published account from the 16th century is the only surviving evidence for much of Coahuiltecan life. Little else remains, except for the countless stone points and tools these resourceful people left behind, the burials which yield clues to archaeology and science, and occasional campsite traces—circles of earth in varying colors revealing where post-holes were dug for shelter, or an impression of a basket placed in moist clay near a hearth and baked into eternity by an evening fire.

*Pronounced "co-ah-weel-TEK-ahn"

Coahuiltecan Indian - c. 1500

Spanish Conquistadores at Río de las Palmas—c. 1520

The earliest-known Spanish attempt at a settlement on the western Gulf Coast was on the *Río de las Palmas*, or "river of palms." A mariner, Alonzo Alvarez de Pineda, found and probed this river during his voyage around the Gulf of Mexico in 1519. That eventful year also saw Cortés launch his conquest of the Aztec empire. A would-be rival of Cortés, Jamaican governor Francisco de Garay, had sent Pineda in hope of finding the long-sought water route to the Far East that would enable him to start his own mainland empire. But the lordly Cortés would tolerate no rivals in "his" Mexico, and Garay's subsequent attempts to colonize met with failure—from mistreatment of native Indians who turned hostile, from bad judgement in the location of settlement sites, from diseases that ravaged the Spanish ranks, and from the power of Cortés' presence. Each of Garay's parties, in turn, struggled to reach Cortés' territory south of the Pánuco River, where survivors were readily persuaded to join the conqueror's forces. Garay himself led the last expedition, which ended as the others had; he later died while a "guest" of Cortés. Earlier, Pineda had led an ill-fated party of his own and was reportedly slain by the fierce Huastecans, his flayed skin and that of his companions displayed on a temple wall.

To conquer the Gulf Coast wilderness, the Spanish brought horses, armor and weapons from Europe. Chain-mail and plate armor were joined by the quilted-cotton jerkins of the native warriors, along with the Spaniards' version in leather. The medieval sword, crossbow and lance remained standard. But a new weapon—the musket, or *arquebus*—roared thunder and belched smoke, terrifying many Indians. (They soon learned, however, that their quick-firing bows and arrows could bring down a gunner before he could reload his bulky one-shot weapon.) And then there was the soldier's invisible armor—his Roman Catholic faith, embodied in the cross or blessed Virgin medallion he wore for divine protection in a dangerous enterprise.

Where was the Río de las Palmas? For many years, popular history—and perhaps wishful thinking—has linked it with the Río Grande itself. Native palms do grow along the river near Brownsville. But recent authoritative studies of Spanish accounts, ships' logs, sailing conditions, and the various rivers which empty into the Gulf suggest strongly that the river charted by Alvarez de Pineda was the *Río Soto la Marina*, with its own palm-lined banks, some 150 miles south.

Cabeza de Vaca in Southern Texas—
c. 1535

Four weather-beaten men, whipped by the southeast wind, view a remarkable sight—a great river, as wide as the Guadalquivir in Spain, from which they had long sailed. Members of a Spanish expedition under one Pánfilo de Narváez, they originally landed on the Florida peninsula in 1528, to explore and claim the coastal lands westward to the Río de las Palmas. But when supplies ran low, the Spaniards built boats to sail along the Gulf coastline to the Río Pánuco and its Spanish settlements. They never made it. A storm wrecked the small craft on the upper Texas Coast, and the survivors were enslaved by Indians. After six years of captivity, four remained—Alvar Nuñez, called Cabeza de Vaca; Alonzo del Castillo; Andrés Dorantes; and a Moorish slave, Estevanico.

Finally making their escape, the four men began an epic, two-year trek through unexplored southern Texas and northern Mexico—until then, unexplored by white men. De Vaca, the acknowledged leader, would later tell of their adventures in his account, *Relación*. Historians still debate their route, interpreted several possible ways from de Vaca's narrative. What is known for certain is that they first headed south, toward the Río Pánuco. Crossing what is now South Texas, they were greeted warmly by Coahuiltecan Indian tribes, who regarded them with awe as shamans for their medical knowledge and healing abilities. Committed to memory, the four castaways' observations would form the first—and, in most cases, the only—primary documentation for Coahuiltecan culture before it succumbed to later Spanish colonization.

Crossing the wide river which reminded de Vaca of the one at Seville, they continued south until they saw mountains. Advised by Indians, perhaps, to avoid the desolate coastal country further on, they turned west, into the unknown heart of North America. After all, the Pacific and its coastal Spanish towns lay fairly close by—or so it was then believed. Helped and succored by friendly Indians, they walked on, becoming so acculturated to the native peoples that their re-acceptance by other Spaniards later on proved difficult. In time, they arrived once more at a river—the Río Grande around present-day Presidio, Texas—and went southwest, for the Pacific Coast settlements. Found, at last, by an astounded group of soldiers, the four castaways were escorted to Mexico City, where they told their amazing story. Their joint report and de Vaca's later *Relación* fired Spanish imaginations with visions of empire and treasure, and led to major exploration of the present-day American Southwest and Southeast.

The river "as wide as the Guadalquivir" was, in all probability, the lower Río Grande, somewhere in what is now Starr or Zapata counties—making de Vaca and his companions the first Europeans to see and describe this vast, arid region. The interpretation of their route used here is mainly that of Alex D. Krieger, whose unpublished thesis (1955) is regarded by many as the most accurate reconstruction of de Vaca's trek.

Cabeza de Vaca in southern Texas, c. 1535

"English Wanderers" on Texas Soil— c. 1570

If Cabeza de Vaca's story is among the most famous in New World history, the trek of the "English wanderers" is perhaps the least known. Yet their tale is no less amazing: how a fight in 1568 between a few English ships and a Spanish fleet in Vera Cruz left one vessel *inglés* sinking, while its crew was transferred onto another; how the English commander, John Hawkins, saw no choice but to maroon the extra men in what is now Tamaulipas, lest the overloaded ship founder on its return voyage; how some 130 men, taken ashore, struck out into the coastal wilderness—many to be captured and imprisoned by the Spanish, others to be killed by Indians, and still others, perhaps, to adopt Indian ways and take up with Coahuiltecan tribes; and how three iron-willed castaways—David Ingram, Richard Browne and Richard Twide—emerged from the interior at New Brunswick, Canada over a year later to tell their story.

They had walked, they said, northward, crossing a river they named "River of May" (for the time of year), and had made their way steadily, month by month, around the coastal regions of eastern North America, helped and guided along by friendly natives. Ingram's account of their journey was published, stirring as much English interest in New World exploration as Cabeza de Vaca's narrative had done for the Spanish. Within a few years, the first attempts were made to establish English settlements on the mainland of what would later be known as the United States.

And what was that "River of May" the Englishmen had spoken of? From David Ingram's account, it was almost certainly the Spaniards' *Río Bravo del Norte*—the Río Grande.

"English Wanderers" on Texas soil, c. 1570

Don Luís de Carvajal—c. 1585

Among the first Europeans to enter the *Seno Mexicano* with a purpose was one Luis de Carvajal, an old frontier hand who well knew the region and its native peoples. He had come to New Spain years before, and made a reputation for exploits along the Gulf coast. Over 70 of John Hawkins' castaway sailors were rounded up by Carvajal, a feat for which he was rewarded with a captaincy. Some time later, in the early 1570s, he led an expedition to chastise the coastal Indians suspected of killing the survivors of a Spanish treasure fleet, wrecked on Padre Island in 1554. On this trek, Carvajal is thought to have crossed the *Río Bravo del Norte*, or *Río Grande*; if so, he became the first known Spanish subject to enter what is now the Rio Grande Valley from the south. (Cabeza de Vaca may have approached the Río Grande from the north.)

By 1580 Carvajal had secured royal permission to form a new province, Nuevo León, with himself as governor and captain-general. He and his adventurers roamed what is now Tamaulipas, enslaving Indians to work the mines in his province. The slave-catching raids may have extended to the Río Grande. But Carvajal also violated the jurisdictions of neighboring administrators, and in time his excesses and cruelty to Indians drew unwelcome attention from the Viceroy—and the Inquisition.

For Carvajal was of Jewish descent. His parents were both *conversos*: two of the thousands of Sephardic Jews to whom the Crown and the Church had given a choice—convert to Christianity or be exiled (or worse). Raised a Roman Catholic, Carvajal remained one; but several family members reverted, becoming "crypto-Jews", practicing their ancestral faith in secret. Subsequently, many conversos and crypto-Jews settled in Carvajal's province. Around 1590, Carvajal was arrested and taken to Mexico City. Charged with administrative misdeeds (it was not the first time, but until then, he had managed to escape punishment), he was also accused of heresy. He gave up several family members to the Inquisition; but this attempt to redeem himself was futile. He died in prison in 1590.

Despite his reputation as a bully and an enslaver of Indians, Carvajal earned his place in lower Río Grande history. This Portuguese conquistador helped broaden Spanish knowledge of the Seno Mexicano, and opened Nuevo León to settlers, including conversos and crypto-Jews, whose many descendants are among the Hispanic population of Tamaulipas and South Texas.

Don Luis de Carvajal - c. 1585

Dutch Intruders on the lower Río Grande—c. 1630

By the late 1500s, Spain was embroiled in struggles with European rivals for control of the New World and its fabulous treasures. In a series of on-again, off-again conflicts stretching over 100 years, the Spanish fought bloody wars against the English, French and Dutch, whose far-sailing privateers, or "sea dogs," hounded Spanish treasure fleets and settlements in the Caribbean and the Gulf of Mexico. Their ever-bolder incursions into the Gulf, which Spain regarded as its private sea, sounded a warning throughout *Nueva España*.

With a flair for sea-borne raiding that surpassed even that of the English, the Hollanders ransacked towns and burned ships from Yucatán to Vera Cruz, all the while exploring and charting the Western Gulf. In the 1630s, Nuevo León heard Indian reports of strange white men on the coast of the *Seno Mexicano*—bearded, blonde men with red legs and sashes who wore helmets. Their ships had big guns that roared with thunder. An alarmed governor sent an expedition to find the intruders—probably the feared *holandeses*. The Cerralvo force, led by Jacinto García de Sepulveda, is believed to have crossed the Río Grande into the present-day Hidalgo County area, headed for the coast. Encountering hostile natives, they withdrew. So, apparently, did the intruders, who may well have probed the Río Grande itself; the "Great River" was already well known to those who sailed the western Gulf. In any case, these "red-leg" invaders, and others like them, by their very presence, prompted further Spanish exploration of the coastal country.

Dutch intruders on the Lower Rio Grande – c. 1630

Ganadero *Español del* Nuevo Reino de León—c. 1650

On his second voyage of discovery, Columbus brought cattle and horses, thus planting in the New World an age-old Spanish way of life. But there was a difference. On the vast plains, plateaus and coastal regions of *Nueva España*, stock-raising from horseback quickly became a major industry, on a scale unknown elsewhere. By the 1600s, the horses and cattle brought by Cortés and others had multiplied into many thousands, and ranching had spread to the farthest frontiers. On *haciendas* or ranches in Nuevo León, stockmen—*ganaderos*—worked their herds of horses and cattle on the Sierra Madre slopes and hills. On the unfenced open ranges, livestock wandered far; many escaped into the wild, giving rise to vast herds of wild cattle and horses, called *cimarrones*, that for 200 years roamed what would later become northern Tamaulipas and southern Texas. The Nuevo León ranchers and their *vaqueros*, or cowboys, may well have pursued runaway stock as far north as the Río Grande and beyond.

This ganadero's clothing, cloak, and feathered hat reflect the popular European styles of the times. Tools of his trade include a saddle of Moorish descent (itself an irony, as the Moors—like the Jews—had also been banished from Spain); a coiled rope, called a *reata*, made of braided horsehair or rawhide; and the ubiquitous *garrocha*, or prod-pole, with its iron tip. His boots, puffed and slashed, are thrust into heavy iron stirrups, which help to secure him in the saddle while galloping along. Across the saddle is a heavy leather drape that protects his legs from thorny brush.

Ganadero español del Nuevo Reino de León
c. 1650

Sargento Mayor Alonso de León's Expedition—c. 1687

In the 1680s, alarming news reached Mexico City. A French colony, under the cavalier LaSalle, had landed on the Gulf coast of New Spain. The long-feared foreign incursion onto the mainland had begun. There was only one course of action to take—the intruders must be found and destroyed! Government wheels turned swiftly, and an expedition was organized at Monterrey. In command was Sergeant-Major Alonzo de León, and like his father for whom he was named, he was an old frontier hand.

De León set out in 1686 with orders to find the French, who were somewhere north of the Río Bravo. His column rode north to the river, then followed its south bank eastward to the Gulf. Finding no LaSalle, they returned to Monterrey. A second attempt was made the following year, also under de León. This time he crossed the Río Grande, probably near present-day Roma, and followed the river's north bank, again to the Gulf. It was said that the French had settled on a bay, and so, de León's force rode northward, skirting the tidal flats and marshes along the Laguna Madre. They went as far as Baffin Bay, before turning back.

In Madrid and Mexico City, nervous officials wondered, "Where *is* LaSalle?" Even a sea-borne attempt to find him had failed. Finally, a third land expedition—again, led by de León—swung northwest and crossed into what is now Texas at Del Rio, and made its way east, passing near San Antonio and on to the coast. Near Matagorda Bay they found the charred ruins of LaSalle's Fort St. Louis, abandoned much earlier, its inhabitants having fled or been killed by Indians. LaSalle himself had been shot by one of his own men on his way to Louisiana.

With the French threat ended, New Spain took steps to prevent its recurrence. Again the Crown called upon de León, who in 1690—a year after finding LaSalle's fort—led an expedition into eastern Texas to establish the first Spanish settlement and mission in that outermost frontier of Nueva España.

De León's written reports of his expeditions gave the Spanish some of their first detailed knowledge of the landscape, environment and native peoples of what later became northern Tamaulipas and South Texas. To check his position in an uncharted wilderness, he used an astrolabe, a circular navigation instrument also used at sea. With helmets and breastplates, chain mail and leather armor, and lances and banners held high, his expeditions must have been a stirring sight as they followed the Río Grande—foretelling the colonization that would come some 70 years later.

Sargento Mayor Alonso de León's expedition, c. 1687

Cattle Coming into Texas—c.1690

Just when the Spanish first brought cattle and horses across the Río Grande is not known for certain. It is known that Alonso de León's expedition of 1690 brought along droves of horses and cattle, leaving some animals at river crossings, in hope of starting wild herds that could benefit later travelers. When de León searched along the Río Grande and lower Texas coast earlier, some runaway livestock from *haciendas* in Nuevo León may have already been there.

By the late 1600s, Indians had learned to prize the horse, and had begun raiding into northern New Spain to capture horses and cattle. Some of these animals inevitably escaped, propagating in the region's brush country and grasslands. And it is not unlikely that occasional forays north of the Río Grande were made by stockmen from Cerralvo and elsewhere in Nuevo León in the final years of the 17th century.

Pushing northward into the Río Grande country with livestock brought about more changes for the *ganadero*. Thorns on almost every plant called for more protection for a rider's legs—knee-high boots, leather *tapaderas* for stirrups, and leather thigh covers, fore-runners of cowboys' chaps. Armor was gradually disappearing; breastplates and chain mail could still ward off arrows, but wide-brim hats—ancestors of the sombrero and Stetson—were replacing helmets and older-style caps.

Saddles, also, were changing. This rider's *silla* has a high extension in front, turning inward slightly at its base. It is for the *reata*, or rope, he uses to catch horses and cattle. When the loop is tossed and pulls tight, the other end is firmly wrapped around the extension, an early version of the saddle horn. Also hanging from the saddle is a leather water bottle. In the driver's hand is a crescent-shaped "hocking spear," or *desjarretadera*, used to bring down a running cow by hamstringing it.

Cattle coming into Texas - c. 1690

Don Joseph de Escandón y Elguera, Conde de la Sierra Gorda—A.D. 1749

On September 3, 1746, the Viceroy of New Spain appointed Don José de Escandón as governor of the new province of *Nuevo Santander*—the sprawling region known today as Tamaulipas and southern Texas. Under his direction, the vast area between the Río Pánuco and the Río Grande was successfully colonized. It marked the beginning of permanent European settlement along the lower Río Grande.

Born in the Santander region of northern Spain, in the village of Soto la Marina, Escandón pursued a military and government career from an early age. As an army cadet, he came to New Spain and served in the Yucatán, fighting Indians and the British. In 1721, he went to Querétaro, and for 20 years he helped pacify and settle la *Sierra Gorda*—the mountainous region later called *Sierra Madre Oriental*. Escandón subdued hostile Indians and founded villages and missions—valuable practical experience for the great endeavor to come.

The Crown requested proposals for colonizing *Nueva España*'s last frontier, between the Sierra Gorda and the Gulf of Mexico. Rugged and forbidding, the region had long defied settlement. Its desolate coast could still invite foreign intrusion (there were still uneasy memories of LaSalle). Colonization would bring a permanent Spanish presence and might deter invasion. Escandón drew upon his frontier experience, as well as his genius for organization, and submitted his plan. The Crown approved and named him governor.

In 1747, Escandón led a massive survey of his new province. Seven military columns, or *tropas*, set out from various points of its perimeter, intending to meet at the mouth of the Río Bravo. The *tropas* recorded the landscape, topography, plant life, water, and other resources which would impact the settlers. Sites for towns and missions were also noted. Armed with this information, Escandón mapped out the actual colonization, and in 1749 it began. Within three years, the country from the Pánuco to the Río Grande was successfully occupied. Escandón himself paid for much of the enterprise. For his loyal service and untiring efforts, the Crown bestowed upon Escandón the title of *Conde de la Sierra Gorda*, or Count of Sierra Gorda, in 1749, and named him a Knight of Santiago, Spain's highest military order.

El Ex.mo Sr. Don Joseph de Escandón y Elguera, Conde de la Sierra Gorda, Caballero de la Orden de Sant.go Coronel del Regimiento de Querétaro, Then.te de Capitán General de Sierragorda, sus Misiones, Presidios y Fronteras y Lugar Then.te del Ex.mo Sr. Virrey de ésta Nueva España en dha. Costa. A.D. 1749.

Pobladores *with Escandón—c.1750*

To settle Nuevo Santander, Escandón recruited the people he knew best—hardy frontier folk of the Sierra Gorda itself. Self-reliant and toughened to spartan living, they were well-suited to the rigorous job of bringing Spanish civilization into a defiant wilderness. For incentives, Escandón's plan offered that most precious commodity—land—and relief from taxes. For defense from Indians they would have to rely mostly on themselves; regular military troops in numbers sufficient to guard the area were not available (or affordable). Escandón believed that these ranchers and farmers would fight willingly enough if their families, homes and holdings were at stake. Some 500 families from Nuevo León and Coahuila answered the call and spearheaded the colonization of Nuevo Santander. These founders—called *pobladores*, or populators—established 14 initial settlements, including those along the Río Grande: Camargo, Reynosa, Mier, Revilla, Laredo and Dolores. Of these, Revilla, now known as Guerrero Viejo, and Dolores were eventually abandoned. The others still flourish.

Livelihoods for the colonists included ranching, which dominated the more arid northern region, and farming, more common in the south and west. Horses outnumbered cattle, and sheep were most numerous of all. Hides, tallow, dried beef, mutton and wool were produced and sold. From farms came cotton, corn, beans, pumpkins, *chiles* and other crops. Salt from El Sal del Rey salt lake and other *salinas* was valued highly as a meat and fish preservative. It was also used in industrial processes, and in making gunpowder. Mines in the western mountains yielded gold, silver and lead. Trade routes linked the province together and allowed the colonists to exchange products with neighboring regions.

Villas, or villages, were the basic units of settlement and government. In layout, most were typically Spanish—a church and municipal house fronting on a square *plaza*, surrounded by streets, houses and shops. Beyond lay fields (irrigated, if near a stream or river) and grazing lands. Ranching villages often were more spread out. Civil and military authority was held by a village *capitán*, responsible to Escandón. Although the population of Nuevo Santander grew, the basic patterns of settlement and ways of life remained the same for many years.

vaquero de Nuevo Santander—c. 1750

Ranching in the province of Nuevo Santander depended, ultimately, on the *vaquero*, the mounted "cow-herd" who rode the open ranges in every kind of weather, chasing cows, rounding up cows and calves, branding and cropping, and in later years, driving herds to distant places. Here, a lone *vaquero*, working cattle near the Río Grande, eases his horse down to the river's edge for a welcome drink. His clothing and gear are a mix of the practical and the decorative—from a simple shirt and straw *sombrero* to the elaborate motifs in saddle leather and iron cross-stirrups. On his boots are large-rowel spurs, the very symbols of his calling, and a source of intense pride. His horse wears a bridle and reins of braided leather, a picket-rope tied loosely around the animal's neck. Saddle-bags, gourd canteen, an *espada*, or sword, and blanket roll serve the vaquero's basic needs. His long prod-pole encourages reluctant cattle to keep moving. Riding along easily to the music of his jingling spurs and creaking leather, his appearance is a testament to the Spanish appreciation for fine craftsmanship, even in the most humble objects.

VAQUERO DE NUEVO SANTANDER - C - 1750

Taking Formal Possession of Land— c. 1760

One of the main incentives to colonize Nuevo Santander was Escandón's offer of land ownership, through his position as governor. Ceremonies to signify the formal possession of land granted by the Crown followed age-old rituals. An official would read aloud the necessary documents, and a priest would bless the land. At times he would take the hand of the grantee and lead him around the tract, while the grantee pulled grass and tossed stones or clods of earth. He could also offer water to the officials and their horses. All of these rituals symbolized the new owner's intent to clear the land as needed, work it, and share its bounty with others. Thus, the grantees and their families asserted true possession in the eyes of the Church and state.

Taking formal possession of land.
c. 1760

Surveyors, Upper Valley Region—c. 1767

Along the Río Grande, the actual northern line of settlement in Nuevo Santander, confusion over land ownership and dispersal began soon after colonization and grew for some 20 years. It was noted by a royal *visita*, or inspection in 1757, but the problem continued. At Escandón's urging, the Viceroy ordered another visita in 1767 to survey and apportion lands. With the help of surveyors, the Judge Commissioner established a system of land ownership based on years of residence in the province. Special regard was given to those of many years' inhabitation, more familiar with the region, and with a greater personal investment. The Commission divided lands among farming, ranching and Church interests. Along streams and rivers, *porciones* were granted—long, narrow strips bordering the water like fringe on a jacket, giving each grantee precious access to pure water for his animals and crops. From the *visita general* of 1767 date many land grants which have figured in lower Río Grande history ever since.

Surveying in colonial times was not the exact science of today. Those performing it used a mixture of frontier methods and newer techniques—from long strips of cowhide which functioned as measuring lines, to metal chains marked in *varas*, the standard unit of land measurement, and the ancestors of the optical transit. Errors in location, reliance on perishable natural features like trees and stumps, stretched hide-lines, the pacing of distances, and other inexactnesses caused a welter of overlapping and conflicting boundaries and claims which have kept real estate lawyers busy, attempting to untangle them, to this day.

Surveyors - Upper Valley region. c. 1767

Spanish Colonial Frontier Dragoons on Patrol in Nuevo Santander—c. 1770

By 1700 the unmatched mobility and power of the horse was transforming the Indian's way of life, including warfare. Nuevo Santander and other parts of New Spain were in frequent danger from raids by mounted Apache and Comanche warriors. Defense, thus, was a routine part of life for Escandón's colonists. To help save the expense of large numbers of royal troops, the settlers were expected to bear arms when necessary, as militia. Most *villas* had about a dozen of these citizen-soldiers, under the village *capitán's* authority. But some regular cavalry were essential to patrol the vast distances and give chase to marauders. These troops were *dragónes*, or dragoons—men in padded leather armor and broad-brimmed hats who wielded short-barrel muskets and *machete*-like swords, but whose weapon of choice was the age-old lance. By 1770, they patrolled the province's northern regions from *presidios* at La Bahía, Monterrey, Cerralvo and Cadereyta. Although too few in number to halt the Indian raids, the dragoons gave an extra measure of security to the frontier, and many a settler could sleep a little easier at night knowing that these soldiers of the King were on guard.

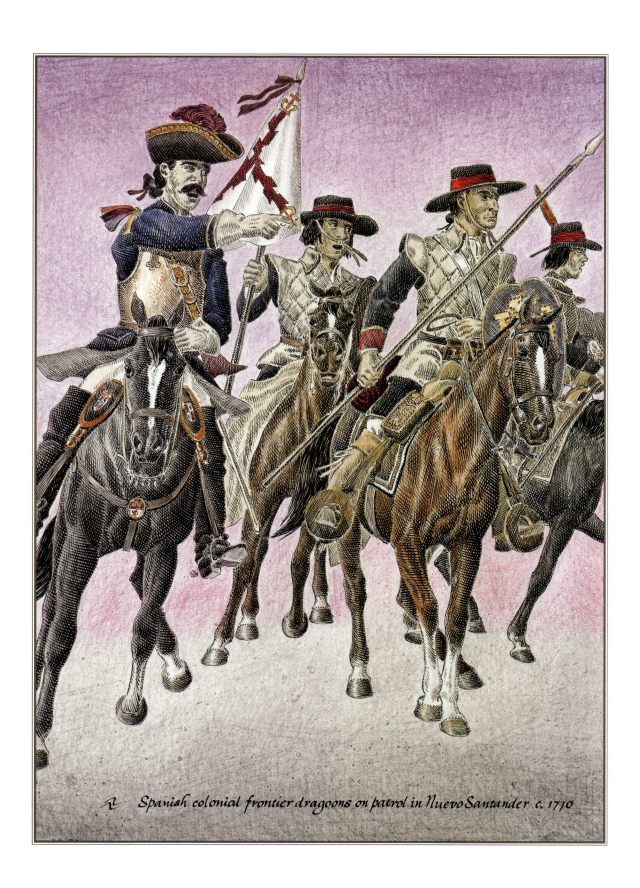
Spanish colonial frontier dragoons on patrol in Nuevo Santander c. 1770

Spanish Colonial Era Cattle Drive— c. 1776

To the Spanish colonial rancher, cattle were valued mainly for their hides, which yielded both *cuero crudo*, or rawhide, and leather of infinite uses, as well as the hard white fat called tallow that was used for candles, soap and grease. Beef very often was consumed on the ranch, mostly in the form of *carne seca*, or dried meat, which would keep for a long time. Not until the 1770s did it become profitable for cattlemen in Nuevo Santander to begin driving herds to distant markets, primarily in the military *presidios* to the south and southwest. Further north, ranchers around the Río Nueces and Río San Antonio areas began driving cattle to Spanish Louisiana.

By then, the British-American colonists were locked in their struggle to overthrow English rule. With the British army and navy heavily engaged with the Americans, Madrid saw an opportunity to retake Florida and other possessions that had been surrendered to England in earlier wars. Spain declared war on England and organized an expedition to wrest away Florida. At the helm was Bernardo de Galvéz, military officer and governor of Louisiana, the expedition's jumping-off place. To feed his great numbers of troops, Galvéz ordered cattle to be driven from Texas to New Orleans. Ranges in the Río San Antonio and Río Nueces regions provided most of the animals. Both the drive and the expedition succeeded, and Florida again belonged to Spain. British troops and ships required to meet the Spanish invasion were pulled away from the American war, relieving pressure on George Washington's army. Thus did Galvéz's expedition, fed by Texas cattle, contribute to the Americans' triumph over the British and to the end of the Revolutionary War.

Sp. Colonial-era cattle drive · c.1776

Spanish Colonial Era Mesteñeros— c. 1780

By the late 1700s, large herds of wild horses roamed the northern regions of Nuevo Santander. Descended from animals which had run away from ranches, these wiry little equines were well-adapted to the broad prairies and dense thickets. As ranching spread further north from the original Río Grande frontier, the job of mustanging was born. The word "mustang" is derived from the Spanish name for wild horses—*mesteños*. Men who specialized in catching them were known as *mesteñeros*. Riding mustangs themselves, these "mustangers" swung their *reatas* of braided rawhide to catch horses, and held them in brush *corrales*, or pens. Hundreds of mustangs were rounded up this way each year for use in ranching or in trade. The colonial ranchers were not the only riders of mustangs, though. Nomadic bands of Indians, such as Lipan Apaches and Comanches, were also mustangers.

A century later, the remnants of the wild-horse herds could still be seen in South Texas, their freedom to roam ever-diminishing with the advent of the barbed wire fence. By 1900, they, along with those legendary mesteñeros, had disappeared from the landscape altogether.

Sp. Colonial-era "Mesteñeros" c.1780

Caporal *(Cowboys' Foreman) — c. 1780*

In the late 1700s new grants were made for lands bordering the long, narrow bay known as *Laguna Madre,* in what are now Cameron and Willacy counties. The intent behind these large grants was to establish ranching and settlement in areas once avoided because of hostile Indians. Influential citizens of older towns like Reynosa received the grants, agreeing to stock them and bring in settlers. But the coastal grants were many miles from the river towns, and most grantees chose not to occupy their new lands themselves. Instead they employed foremen, or *caporales*, to supervise the ranches.

As elsewhere in Nuevo Santander, horses were more important than cattle, and the open grasslands provided ample grazing for wild horses and Spanish stock alike. On cool autumn or spring days, with the sun overhead and the sea wind ruffling manes and tails, a caporal's life must have seemed pleasant, indeed.

Caporal (Cowboys' Foreman) c.1780

Salt Miners—Salineros— at El Sal del Rey Lake—c.1790

The shallow salt lakes north of the Río Grande became an important resource for Nuevo Santander. Salt, like other minerals, was considered royal property; the most famous of the lakes, in fact, was called *El Sal del Rey*—literally "the salt of the King." Under the careful scrutiny of government officials, the salt could be mined privately in return for a tax payment, equal in value to about 1/5 of what was taken out. As a natural preservative for meat and fish, and as a seasoning, salt was high in demand throughout New Spain. Much of the supply came from El Sal del Rey, *La Sal Vieja* and other *salinas* on long pack-trains of mules, the salt packed in coarsely woven bags.

Like the Indians before them, the colonial *salineros* needed few tools to mine salt. Hoes and shovels were used to dig and scrape loose the white crystals, which were then piled to dry on the lake shore. The dried salt was then shoveled into the transport bags, which were sewn shut with thick twine and heavy needles, and tied onto the mules. Bearing the brunt of this laborious job were the *mestizos* and Indians, miners and muleteers, who risked death from Indian attacks as they guided their animals and precious cargo southward to the Río Grande and beyond.

The salt trade continued well into the 20th century, with oxcarts, wagons, and finally, motor trucks replacing the Spaniards' faithful mules. Mining at El Sal del Rey ended around the time of World War II.

Salt miners – "salineros" – at El Sal del Rey Lake – c. 1790

Franciscan Visiting Upper Valley Settlements—c. 1800

Arriving with Escandón's colonists were Franciscan priests, who planted the Roman Catholic Church on the lower Río Grande. Always few in number, the *padres* organized congregations in the early towns and founded missions for the Indians. As ranching and settlement spread north of the river, the churchmen traveled ever further to administer to far-flung colonists. Often these remote villagers and ranch folk were visited only once a year by a priest, who would perform baptisms, sanctify marriages, hear confession, and bestow their blessing upon people, their dwellings, and their all-important animals.

For their constant travels, the padres walked on sandaled feet, accompanied perhaps by an Indian neophyte. Patient *burros* carried sacramental vessels packed for transport, along with food and water. Wherever they went, it took only a makeshift altar and the intonation of prayer to turn a patch of cactus and dirt into a place of worship. The blue-gray robes of Franciscans played as great a role as the chain mail and armor of Spanish explorers in firmly establishing the civilization of New Spain in this isolated frontier.

Franciscan visiting Upper Valley settlements - c.-1800

Colonial Sheep Herder and Family—
c. 1800

In Spanish and later Mexican times, sheep and goats outnumbered all other livestock. The centuries-old Spanish tradition of sheep-raising was easily transported to *Nueva España* by Escandón's settlers, who brought sheep and goats along with their horses and cattle. Wool from *las ovejas* (the sheep) found its way to distaffs, spinning wheels and looms across Nuevo Santander and into neighboring regions. Warm blankets, *rebozos* (shawls), *ponchos* and *sarapes* could ward off the cold of winter "northers" and the chill of higher lands in the Sierra Gorda. Sheep also provided meat for the pot, as did goats, or *cabras*; barbecued goat—*cabrito*—is still a favorite dish in the region. Goats also yielded milk and soft fleece for spinning.

The use of sheep and goat products was efficient and economical. In sparsely-populated regions these smaller animals would be quickly consumed, where a butchered cow might go to waste. Every year, at shearing time, the *pastores,* or shepherds, and their families rounded up their wooly charges and drove them together near homes of *jacál,* or mud-plastered brushwood, *adobe* bricks, or the limestone blocks known as *sillares*. Even more so than the neighing of horses or the "bawing" of cattle, the bleat of sheep and goats was long the true natural music of the lower Río Grande.

Colonial - sheepherder and family, c. 1800

Frontier Hispanic Family Defending their Home—c. 1810

Throughout the colonial period, and indeed well after it, Indian raids scourged Nuevo Santander. Resenting the white men's intrusion, and coveting his livestock, hard-riding bands of Lipan Apaches and Comanches burned homes, killed settlers and stole horses, cattle and sheep. Villages and ranches alike, were hit; men, women and children fell to arrow, lance and war-club. Cries and curses of the attacked mingled with the war whoops of the attackers, the roar of musket fire, and the pounding of hooves, as the livestock were driven away. When a raid ended, the Indians withdrew—to mountain strongholds in the west, or to the wilderness north of the Río Grande. So it went, year after year.

Escandón had hoped that his colonists would be able to defend themselves adequately, without the expense of a large military force in his province. Scarcely 130 mounted regular troops were assigned in 1749, to be divided up among the villages. In addition, a certain number of colonists were enrolled as citizen-soldiers or militia. But they were seldom enough, and despite repeated attempts to bring it under control, the Indian menace remained far longer than expected. The settlers could only stand fast, trusting in their weapons and in their God, to help them survive the trial.

Lipan Apache Warriors—c. 1820

Few words struck terror into the hearts of borderland settlers as did "Apache!" From Texas to Arizona, they were feared as devils on horseback, and the implacable enemies of the encroaching white man—no matter his language. Displaced from their homelands on the Staked Plains of Texas, New Mexico and further north, Apache groups migrated to the southeast, south and southwest. The eastern Apaches, known as *Lipans*, entered the region between the Río Grande and the Río Nueces—today's South Texas—and from it, bands of warriors raided towns and ranches in Nuevo Santander. Horses and other livestock, were favorite targets; saddles, muskets and powder horns were also taken on occasion—even children, to be adopted into tribes. Lipans continued their forays well into the 1800s. At times, they had to compete for plunder with those who had originally displaced them—the even more warlike Comanches, whose annual thrusts into northern New Spain were times of universal dread. Not until long after Spanish rule were the Apaches and Comanches corralled into reservations, forever ending their raids.

Mexican Insurgentes— Independence Fighters on the Northern Frontier—c. 1820

A mounting discontent with Spanish rule erupted in 1810, when Father Miguel Hidalgo gave his *grito* (shout) in Dolores and called the Mexican people to revolt. His shout echoed loudly on the northeastern frontier, where a population living in near-isolation from Mexico City had long depended on themselves and their arms for survival. With the recent examples of the British-Americans and the French to consider, many on the lower Río Grande decided that their time for freedom had also come. Among the earliest and most dedicated champions of the Mexicans' rebellion against Spain were the brothers Gutiérrez de Lara of Revilla, now known as *Guerrero Viejo*.

José Antonio Gutiérrez de Lara was, like Hidalgo, a priest. He had traveled the lower Río Grande frontier, agitating for revolt; after it began, he continued his self-appointed mission, helping to sustain the people's morale when failure seemed, at times, certain. But better known was his brother, José Bernardo. A merchant and blacksmith, he worked tirelessly for the rebellion, and almost kept it alive himself after Hidalgo's peasant army was scattered and its leader shot in 1811. He went to Washington, D.C. to solicit military and financial aid; the Americans were willing to help, but their terms—mainly to possess Texas—were not acceptable. Going next to New Orleans, then a hotbed for soldiers of fortune, José Bernardo raised a mixed army of foreigners, invaded Texas, forced the Spanish authorities out of San Antonio, and established the first Republic of Texas in 1813. Spanish retaliation was swift, and four months later, the new republic fell. José Bernardo escaped and remained active in border-revolt activities. After independence was won in 1821, both of the brothers remained active in the establishment of the Republic of Mexico and left an undying legacy for the people of the lower Río Grande.

Mexican "insurgentes" – independence fighters – on the northern frontier, c. 1820

Ganadero *and* Vaquero— Mid-Valley Area—c. 1830

Mexican cattlemen of the early 1800s, like their Spanish forebears, took great pride in their dress and horse trappings. For the *ganadero*, or rancher, his personal appearance was a symbol of prestige and authority, from his large-roweled spurs to his wide-brimmed hat. *Vaqueros*, or cowboys, dressed more simply, but with no less pride. Their clothing and gear were born to meet the demands of stock tending from horseback, in a land of thorny plants and little water. Despite adversities like floods, drought and Indian raids, the Spanish and Mexican ranching tradition survived, leaving a permanent mark on the cultural and economic history of the lower Río Grande.

By the time of Mexican Independence, in the 1820s and 30s, regular contact between the Río Grande frontier and Europe had slowed to a trickle. Spanish-inspired Mexican styles were of "arrested" Baroque type. From the carefully stamped *tapaderas,* or stirrup covers, of this ganadero, to the double-ruffled short-sleeved *chaqueta* of the vaquero, the styles of earlier decades remained an integral form of expression. Yet changes were in the wind. Well to the north, in the Mexican state of Texas, the call for rebellion would once again be heard—this time, among the *americanos* who had begun to colonize the region under an arrangement with the central government in the 1820s. Now there was dissatisfaction with Mexican rule, and increasingly, there were calls for change to a more democratic way—by force of arms, if necessary.

Within a few years, these "Texians" would win their independence with rifles and cannons—in bloody battles at the Alamo, Goliad and San Jacinto. A new Republic of Texas would be declared, with its boundary at the Río Grande. Uncertain times would begin for the ranch and town folk along the river, whose old way of life was about to change forever.

"Ganadero and Vaquero - Mid-Valley area. - c. 1830"

Texan Adventurers (Filibusters)— c. 1840s

Texas' independence from Mexico began a long period of uneasy relations between the two republics and their peoples. Claimed as sovereign territory by both was the vast, rolling country between the Río Grande and the Río Nueces. Attacks and counter-attacks by both sides flared across this "Nueces Strip," as Mexican forces struck into Texas, and Texans launched invasions of Mexican soil. A pattern was set for distrust, warfare and death that would fester for many years along the border.

Such an environment attracted scores of adventurers, or *filibusteros* (free-booters), from the U.S. and other countries, drawn to Texas by the chance to make their fortunes or just to raise hell. Their predecessors had come during the last years of Spanish rule, fomenting revolt among the *Tejanos* and Río Grande settlers. Now a new generation of filibusters rode in, joining such "enterprises" as the Texan invasion of New Mexico, known as the Santa Fe Expedition, and the short-lived "Republic of the Río Grande," in which a mixed force of Hispanic and Anglo adventurers declared the Mexican territory adjoining Laredo to be an independent nation. It was quickly crushed by Mexican forces.

The most famous of the filibustering attempts was the "Mier Expedition," in late 1842. A group of Texan volunteers, disobeying orders from the government, crossed the lower Río Grande and attacked the old colonial town of Mier. They were soon defeated by regular army troops, and marched to imprisonment near Mexico City; survivors later were returned to Texas. After Texas joined the Union in 1845, the deep-rooted cycle of violence and hate along the Texas-Mexico frontier continued for decades—a legacy left behind by those early filibusteros.

Texan adventurers (filibusters) c.-1840

Zachary Taylor's U.S. Army Dragoon Talking to Sarah Borginnis—c. 1846

Among the most memorable characters in the U.S. war with Mexico were a robust Irish woman named Sarah Borginnis, and a teenaged Yankee trooper named Samuel Chamberlain. Standing six feet tall, or better, in her bare feet, Sarah Borginnis was among the women "camp followers" who came as cooks and laundresses with Zachary Taylor's army, from Corpus Christi to the Río Grande. During the Mexicans' bombardment of Taylor's earthwork Fort Texas in early May of 1846, Borginnis courageously tended to wounded men, and generally helped keep up morale. After the U.S. occupation of Matamoros, she opened the first of several barrooms which catered to thirsty American troops, as the army marched into northern Mexico. The soldiers—officers and enlisted, alike—knew and loved this erstwhile saloon-keeper, nurse and compatriot, who could bully as well as coddle, and who, it was said, could out-swear any trooper. After the war, Sarah Borginnis headed further west, following the army. She died in Arizona and was the first woman to be buried with military honors. In the furnace-like heat at Fort Yuma, the soldiers said goodbye to the big Irish woman, whom they had affectionately nicknamed after the world's largest steam ship—the "Great Western."

Sam Chamberlain was a strapping, blonde youth from Massachusetts, who fought the Mexican War as a dragoon. Outfitted with the army's most advanced small arms and unmistakable dark-blue coats with crossed white belts and yellow cap-band of their branch, dragoons were the mounted elite—the heavy "shock troops" who fought in major and minor actions, alike, from the Río Grande to the Valley of Mexico. Chamberlain's outfit was attached to Taylor's army in time for the Battle of *La Angostura*, or *Buena Vista*. Like a number of American soldiers, he wrote an account of his adventures. But unlike others, he illustrated it with his own watercolor pictures, each done by hand for the hand-written memoirs he entitled *My Confession*. Chamberlain's account—which included battles, skirmishes with Mexican guerrillas, sword duels, rescuing damsels and bedroom escapades with *señoritas*—reads more like an adventure novel than a war diary, and some historians doubt its total veracity. But the "ring of truth" is there, and through its lively narrative and detailed miniature paintings, Sam Chamberlain left a unique and valuable perspective of the Mexican War's northern campaign.

Zachary Taylor's U.S. Army Dragoon talking to Sarah Borginnis, c. 1846

Mexican Cavalrymen at the Battle of Buena Vista—c. 1847

By February, 1847, the American army under Zachary Taylor had most of northeastern Mexico under its control. The price in dead and wounded men had been high, yet the campaign to secure the Río Grande and neutralize enemy forces south of it appeared successful. But the fighting was not done yet. General Antonio López de Santa Anna, that most enigmatic figure in Mexican political and military history, was again leading an army northward to strike down the *gringos,* as he had 11 years before. Warned of his approach, Taylor moved his forces south of occupied Saltillo to the fantastically-eroded landscape of gullies and plateaus near Hacienda Buena Vista. The Mexicans called the place *La Angostura*. It was here that the road to Saltillo passed through a narrow defile, and it was here that "Old Rough and Ready," as Taylor was known to his troops, made his stand.

On a cold February 23rd, the two armies clashed in a day-long struggle. With some 15,000 men, Santa Anna attacked Taylor's defensive position, held by about 4,000 troops—mostly volunteers. The combined forces of infantry, cavalry and artillery wreaked fearful havoc, and both armies took a beating. By mid-afternoon, an American defeat seemed certain. A final, magnificent charge by Mexican cavalry, their lances and sabers ready and banners flying, thundered toward the *yanquis* to deliver the crushing blow. Only too late did they realize the trap—they had been drawn into the open end of a wide "V" of Indiana and Mississippi troops, Taylor's last effective force, which now closed around the oncoming horsemen and opened fire. Riders and horses plunged to the ground with terrible carnage. It was the battle's turning point. Santa Anna pulled back his remaining troops as darkness fell. Taylor's exhausted men awoke the next morning to find the enemy gone. A demoralized Santa Anna was taking his army back southward, unwilling or unable to resume the battle—which would have finished Taylor.

On such decisions does the course of history change. With northern Mexico secured, General Scott and his invasion force were able to carry out the campaign from Vera Cruz to the capital, which fell in September of that same year. Had the last Mexican charge at Buena Vista succeeded, the two nations' destinies would have been quite different.

Mexican Cavalrymen at the Battle of Buena Vista, 1847

Steamboat Captain—c. 1850

For over a half-century, steamboats plowed the Río Grande, their paddle wheels churning the waters into a highway. War brought the boats, and trade with Mexico kept them afterward. In 1846, to supply his army in northeastern Mexico, Zachary Taylor procured a fleet of side wheelers from the Ohio, Mississippi, and other rivers. They carried tons of military supplies and provisions, as well as troops, from Matamoros all the way to Camargo and Roma. At war's end, some private interests bought the remaining, well-used boats to carry commercial freight and passengers. Two steamboaters who thus made their mark were Mifflin Kenedy and Richard King; their firm of M. Kenedy & Co. came to dominate—even monopolize—Río Grande traffic, through the 1850s and 60s. Both men also became ranchers on the broad coastal prairies, with King's becoming in time the vast, world-famous ranch that still bears his name.

The golden years of Río Grande steamboating were the 1850s. To the old Mexican War boats were added newer vessels, side wheelers and stern wheelers, that opened the lower Río Grande and northeastern Mexico to foreign trade on a large scale. Manufactured goods of all descriptions brought by sea to Matamoros and the new city of Brownsville, went upriver; most were bound for merchants in the towns and cities of Tamaulipas, Nuevo León and Coahuila. Other goods were off-loaded along the river, at ranch settlements or towns. Among the best customers were the new U.S. Army posts of Fort Brown and Ringgold Barracks (later called Fort Ringgold). Soldiers and their families, weapons and materiel, and the hundreds of assorted items required for frontier military duty rode the steamboats. So did civilians of all kinds—merchants, ranchers, businessmen, government officials, gamblers, and shadowy characters on errands they preferred be kept secret. For as the lower Río Grande and northern Mexico opened to world trade, some foreign governments were taking increasing interest in Mexico's great natural resources. In 1861, France, Spain and England would mount direct military intervention in Mexico, with France remaining longest—establishing a puppet imperial government and opening a long civil war in which the Río Grande would play a strategic role. Yet the daily business of running a steamboat for profit still came first. Here, a well-dressed gentleman and his lady, ready to board a steamboat, chat with a gun-toting skipper, his clothing a mix of surplus military and civilian garb.

Steamboat Captain - c.1850

U. S. Army Lieutenant at Fort Ringgold—c. 1851

From the end of the Mexican War into the 1940s, the U.S. Army maintained forts along the lower Río Grande border. Fort Brown at Brownsville and Fort McIntosh at Laredo anchored the two ends of this often-turbulent region. In the middle was Ringgold Barracks, later re-named Fort Ringgold, at Rio Grande City. Here, under conditions much different from those "back East," many American soldiers learned first-hand about the unique culture and people of the border. Climate and geography would have seemed foreign to these men, but even more so to their wives, who sometimes accompanied them. At least one spouse wrote about her experiences at Ringgold in a small memoir entitled *Following the Drum*. Some aspects of border life did not impress her favorably, but she did recall some pleasant interludes, such as late-afternoon rides with her lieutenant husband, from the post to the town and back, as searing daytime heat gave way to "salubrious" evening breezes.

U.S. Army Lt. at Fort Ringgold - c. 1851

Blacksmith, Ranch Settlement—c.1860

Often overlooked by historians are the craftsmen and ordinary laborers who helped sustain frontier settlements. Along the lower Río Grande, the *herrero,* or blacksmith, was needed by town and ranch folk alike. Depending on his abilities, the smith shod horses, made branding irons, fashioned hardware for doors and windows, and repaired tools. He might also perform more specialized tasks, such as putting new tires on wagon wheels. Few tasks could have been hotter than working a forge during a South Texas summer, but without the blacksmith's iron-working skills, this region would not have been settled.

Nails clenched in his teeth, this herrero prepares to replace a horse's broken shoe. His heavy leather apron protects him from the showers of sparks that fly when his hammer strikes hot iron. Mounted atop a stump is his anvil, with pincers, cutters and other tools hung below. A helper works the big bellows on the forge, where iron is heated until ready for the anvil. Ornate brackets on the porch posts attest to the smith's artistry.

Blacksmith, ranch settlement. - c. 1860

Juan Nepomuceno Cortina's Raiders— c. 1860

CORTINA! Few names have stirred the emotions of the lower Río Grande region like that of Juan Nepomuceno Cortina. A true folk hero among the poorer Mexicans along the river, Cortina led a guerrilla band against Anglos, in retaliation for years of injustices toward the *mexicanos* and *tejanos*. Over a span of some 15 years, Cortina fought the local authorities, the Texas Rangers and the U.S. Army, as well as the French Imperial troops and even the Confederate States forces. His bold defiance of the *gringos* made him very popular among the Mexican people, many of whom joined his band of raiders. The *cortinistas* burned, looted and stole cattle from Brownsville to near Laredo, beginning in 1859. Fights occurred in many places, including Brownsville, Rio Grande City and Carrizzo (later renamed Zapata). Though sometimes defeated and forced to retreat, Cortina was never captured. Some of his men, however, were captured and hanged.

Cortina helped fight the French at the Battle of Puebla in 1862, a victory celebrated throughout Mexico as *El Cinco de Mayo*; later, he did business with them, and with the Confederates during the Civil War years on the Río Grande. When the Union occupied Brownsville, he again switched sides and allied himself with the "boys in blue." *Cortinistas* helped guard Brownsville from attack by Confederates and Imperialists. In later years, "Cheno" appointed himself governor of Tamaulipas (twice), and in the 1870s was back on the border. Accused of being involved in cattle rustling, he was summoned to the capital by Mexican authorities, and lived out his life in southern Mexico. Even today, he is still regarded by many along the border as a "Robin Hood" figure. To others, he was, and continues to be known as "the Red Raider of the Rio Grande." Either way, Juan Cortina and his band of followers left one of the most colorful legacies in the region's annals.

Juan Nepomuceno Cortinas's raiders, c. 1860

Cotton Trade During the Civil War— c. 1863

The lower Río Grande was swept into two civil wars during the 1860s. To the north, the United States and Confederate States were in a death grip, while to the south, Mexico was torn apart by the French intervention. For both conflicts, the river served as a trade corridor, funneling sea-borne supplies and arms into Mexico and Texas, including a torrent of "white gold"—cotton. As the Union blockade closed Southern ports, the Río Grande delta became a "back door" for Confederate commerce. Down the coastal bend, from Texas, Arkansas and Louisiana, came wagon-train loads of cotton, hauled to Brownsville, baled and loaded onto foreign ships offshore. Textile mills in Britain, France and elsewhere in Europe still depended heavily on American cotton. With the tightening of the blockade, the Río Grande became increasingly significant, and by 1863, the cotton trade was flourishing.

To shut off the trade, Union forces invaded the lower Río Grande region late in 1863, occupying Point Isabel, Brownsville and points west, clear to Rio Grande City. But the "back door" was still open. Cotton wagons also headed west, beyond Union reach, and crossed into Mexico at Laredo and Del Rio. The cargoes were baled and hauled toward the coast by road and by steamboats of M. Kenedy & Co., conveniently placed under Mexican registry during the war, and thus immune from Yankee interference. Passing through brokerage houses in Matamoros, the endless torrent of bales streamed into a riverside village called Bagdad. Located next to the Gulf, Bagdad overnight became one of the world's busiest ports. Its warehouses bulged with cotton bound for Europe (and, it should be added, the Union.) Offshore were anchored 200 or more ships at a time, with small boats called "lighters" taking their in-bound cargoes ashore and bringing out cotton. Flags of England, France, Holland, Spain, Belgium, Austria, the German states and other countries rippled from mastheads in the "cotton fleet," which lay in Mexican waters. U.S. Navy captains on blockade ships nearby could only watch in frustration, as Mexico was considered neutral territory in the Civil War.

The cotton trade, while it lasted, was immensely profitable. It made vast fortunes for many; a number of lower Río Grande families trace their wealth back to those times. But like most booms, it finally went bust. By late 1864, the "rebs" had retaken the Valley and re-opened Brownsville, yet the trade slowed down. A cotton glut in Europe and the South's sagging war effort brought decline. By the spring of 1865, the war was over. The conflict in Mexico also ended, and trade along the Río Grande assumed a slower pace. In 1867, a hurricane leveled Bagdad, and within a few years there was little left to mark the frenzied wartime commerce, except for the name by which it is still remembered—*los algodones*, the "cotton times."

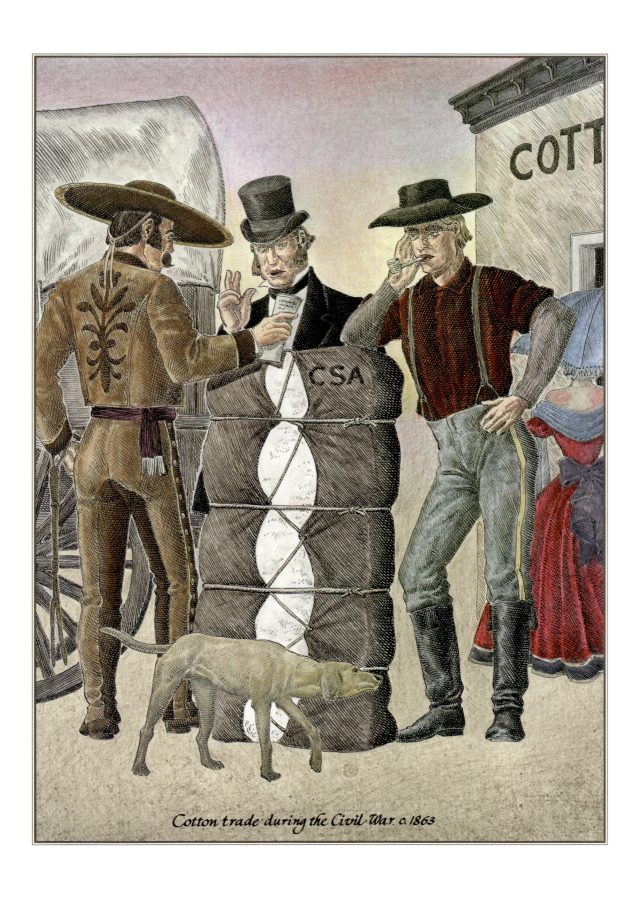
Cotton trade during the Civil War. c. 1863

Confederate Camels at Brownsville—
c. 1864

In the 1850s, the U.S. Army brought camels from the Middle East for trial use in Texas and the Southwest. The War Department wanted to find out if the "ships of the desert" could transport military supplies in the American deserts. In fact, the camels worked well. They could carry sizeable loads over long, arid distances without water. Along with the beasts came Turks to tend them and to teach soldiers the fine art of camel driving. But the troopers, in general, found the animals cantankerous, smelly and mean-tempered—in short, just plain disagreeable. Despite its general success (leaving aside the negative response from troopers), the "Camel Corps" was short-lived. When the Civil War began, the Corps was dissolved and its animals left behind, some of them in Texas.

The Confederates made attempts to use the camels. Salt, of vital importance to the war effort, was mined from *salines* near the Río Grande. Some camels carried salt from El Sal del Rey and La Sal Vieja to San Antonio, across the hot, dry expanse of South Texas. Others found use as cotton transports. With a bale slung on each side, a number of camels made trips down to Brownsville, returning with other cargoes. The camels' demeanor did not impress the city fathers, who passed an ordinance forbidding anyone to walk camels on Brownsville streets. Besides the aforementioned temperament and aroma, the animals also liked to spit on passersby, a habit which did not endear them to the citizenry.

As the war came to an end, the remaining camels were sold or turned loose. For years afterward, there were reports of them in the region. But eventually they disappeared, closing a remarkable chapter in the history of these borderlands.

Confederate camels at Brownsville, c. 1864

Union Army Soldiers at Palmito Ranch, Last Battle of the Civil War—c. 1865

Before the Civil War's end, a large number of freed slaves and other African-Americans were mustered into Union Army regiments. Designated "U.S.C.T.," or "United States Colored Troops," and commanded by white officers, they took up the fight against slavery and secession, and displayed great valor in combat. It seemed fitting that USCTs would fight in the last directed engagement of the war—Palmito Ranch, near Brownsville.

May, 1865. With Confederate strength in the lower Río Grande region shrinking daily through desertions, Union commanders on Brazos Santiago Island planned a march toward Brownsville. Their objective may have been the seizure of cotton for personal profit, or just the gathering of supplies and lumber for the garrison on Brazos. Two regiments of Colored Troops, along with an Indiana regiment and a squad of Texas Cavalry (without horses) made up the force, which numbered about 460. All were infantry. Late on May 12, they encountered enemy scouts near White Ranch and Palmito Ranch, on the river about halfway between Brownsville and the Gulf. Skirmishing continued until nightfall. The next day, the main body of horsemen from Brownsville arrived on the scene with artillery. Late that afternoon, they charged the Union troops and began firing cannons. The Federals returned fire, with casualties on both sides. A number of Union troops were taken prisoner. Deciding that their position could not hold, the Union officers began a withdrawal eastward. Confused maneuvering gave way to order, as the foot soldiers returned to Boca Chica Pass, with Indianans providing a rear guard. Their horses jaded, the Confederates broke off pursuit around sunset, trading the war's last volley of fire with some of the black soldiers. The last battle of the Civil War had ended, as had the war itself—thanks, in part, to the gallant service of the USCTs.

Union Army soldiers at Palmito Ranch, last battle of the Civil War - 1865

Confederate Army Soldiers at the Battle of Palmito Ranch—c. 1865

By the spring of 1865, the Confederacy's fall was only a matter of time. On the Río Grande, military action had almost ceased. The remaining rebel troops in Brownsville waited for the end, their numbers reduced by desertions. Yet, when alerted to the approach of Union soldiers near Palmito Ranch, the Confederate commander, Col. John S. Ford, rallied some 200 cavalrymen and six horse-drawn field guns with their crews and started east. Late on May 13, around 4 p.m., Ford met the enemy. He ordered a charge, accompanied by cannon fire, and before long, the Federals began a withdrawal, back to their fortified positions on Brazos Santiago Island. From across the river, Imperial soldiers watched the action, and appeared ready to assist the Confederates, if needed. In the wartime "stew" of international politics on the Río Grande, the French Imperial regime was openly sympathetic with the Southern cause, while the North supported Benito Juárez in his fight to drive out the French. (Ford's artillery crews reportedly included volunteers from the occupation forces in Matamoros.) Wounded men fell on both sides, but the battle claimed only 3 lives. Among the Confederates' prisoners were a number of soldiers from the United States Colored Troops. Rebel troops back east had been known to abuse or murder black P.O.W.'s, but that did not occur here, and the men later returned to their regiments.

Around sunset, the Confederates' already-jaded horses gave out, and the pursuit ended. A last exchange of gunfire with the Federals marked the end of the war's last battle. Shortly after, Brownsville was surrendered and the last Confederates started for home.

A persistent question about this battle is this: Did either side know that Robert E. Lee had surrendered a month earlier? A likely answer is: Yes, one or both sides probably knew, for such news would have traveled quickly. And Lee's was not the only Confederate army. Others in the Deep South and West did not give up until well after Appomattox.

Confederate Army soldiers at the Battle of Palmito Ranch - c. 1865

The New Beginning

For many Civil War veterans, South Texas was a place to "begin again." Some came to the lower Río Grande country as returners, others as newcomers. Enormous numbers of wild longhorn cattle, which had multiplied during the war, offered to many "Yanks" and Rebs" a chance to get into ranching. The *gringos* began learning from the native *vaqueros,* and developed a few methods of their own. The going was not easy. Besides the thorny brush, heat and often rainless skies, the region was infested with cattle thieves and other outlaws who found it a sanctuary. But the soldiers-turned-ranchers persevered, and they helped build the Texas cattle business into a legendary industry.

This "Johnny Reb," still wearing his artillery uniform and "kepi" cap, surveys his new domain. Carbine and pistol are ready if needed, along with the ever-present gourd canteen. He will soon adopt the clothing of the *vaqueros,* so well suited to their calling, but his saddle is already pure borderlands—from the great wooden horn to the leather toe-fenders, or *tapaderas.*

The New Beginning

French Imperial Forces Along the Río Grande—c. 1865

By 1860, Mexico had drawn the attention of European powers with dreams of colonizing the young republic and exploiting its wealth and resources. French, English and Spanish troops were sent to enforce payment of interest on Mexico's foreign debts, but in 1861, only the French remained. With visions of a Mexican "empire," Napoleon III set up Maximilian as puppet Emperor of Mexico, an action that ignited civil warfare. President Benito Juárez's government went into exile in the north and began a years-long fight to regain control. Aid to Juárez came from the United States; locked in conflict with the Confederacy, Washington feared a possible alliance between French Imperial forces and the Southerners with whom they sympathized. So Lincoln sent arms, ammunition and supplies to Juárez—secretly, since the U.S. was ostensibly neutral. And the Mexican struggle went on.

In 1864, some 5,000 Belgian, Austrian and French troops landed at Bagdad, occupying the south bank of the Río Grande from the Gulf coast to the vicinity of Camargo. Their presence added to the international complexity of the region, in which the forces of the Confederacy, the Union, Cortina and of course, Juárez, were also at work. But Imperial fortunes began to wane, as the *juaristas* inflicted defeats and gained more ground. In 1866, they re-took the lower Río Grande, and the Imperial troops left. The next year, Juárez triumphed, Maximilian was shot, and Mexico began unifying once more.

With their colorful array of uniforms, distinctive "havelocks" to shade the neck from the sun, and mixture of languages, the Imperialist troops brought an exotic presence to the Río Grande. Some had served in Africa, the Crimea and elsewhere. Their influence upon the culture of the region lasted long after them. An echo of the Imperial era is heard in *mariachi* music, which native Mexicans fashioned from music heard at French weddings.

French Imperial forces along the Rio Grande
c. 1865

Mexican Soldiers—c. 1865

With a long and bloody struggle, the Republican armies loyal to President Benito Juárez freed Mexico from the French Imperial occupation. The Mexicans' stunning victory at Puebla on May 5, 1862, stopped the French invasion cold, and forced Napoleon III to commit some 45,000 troops to Mexico. Driven from the south by this massive force, the outnumbered *republicanos* fell back to the north, while the French, Austrian, Belgian and other units occupied much of the country, including the lower Río Grande in 1864. From strongholds in rugged northern regions, the followers of Juárez, the *juaristas,* waged a guerrilla war upon the invaders. Hampered by lack of money and not enough arms or supplies, the Mexicans nevertheless inflicted losses on the Imperialists and harassed them constantly. A trickle of guns and money from a pro-Juárez Washington became a river after the Civil War ended. The juaristas soon had larger forces with better equipment, and began defeating the enemy on his own terms. In the northeast, the important Battle of Santa Gertrudis, fought near Camargo on July 8, 1866, broke Imperial power on the Río Grande. The withdrawal of French forces from Mexico began, leaving "Emperor" Maximilian and his Imperial Mexican army to hold on. Final victory for Juárez came in May 1867, when Querétaro fell. The despised puppet emperor was shot, and in July, the triumphant Juárez and his forces entered Mexico City.

His non-Mexican contemporaries often viewed the juarista soldier with disdain. But as the French were reminded, it is dangerous to underestimate an enemy. The average Republican *soldado* was likely to be an Indian (as was Benito Juárez himself), toughened by life in the field, and a hardened combat veteran. His uniform was often a mixture of French military style and peasant dress, as seen on the infantryman pictured standing. Aside from his frock coat and shako hat, he wears cotton trousers that protrude from under his rolled up army pants. Sandals—*guaraches*—were almost universal. The horseman is an "irregular," a guerrilla lancer of the Río Grande frontier, wearing his *vaquero* garb and sombrero, enjoying a welcome *taza de agua* from a water vendor. Such men won the crucial battle of Santa Gertrudis and drove the *imperialistas* from the Río Grande.

Mexican soldiers - c. 1865

Vaquero *on Trail Drive—c.1870*

Texas' ranching industry grew from Spanish roots, and was nurtured in the country between the Río Grande and the Río Nueces. By the 1870s, cattle driven to railroad "cowtowns" were revitalizing a Texas economy wrecked by the Civil War. Millions of wild longhorn cattle roamed South Texas and the Coastal Bend after the war. Many veterans and others began ranching by rounding up longhorns and branding them. Pre-war trail drives had taken "beeves" to Missouri, but fears of tick-borne "Texas fever"—a fatal livestock disease to which the longhorn carriers were immune—closed the old eastern routes. Railroads pushing across Nebraska and Kansas had the answer. They built shipping pens and invited Texans to bring their herds. The rest is history.

By 1870, endless streams of cattle went "up the trail" in annual drives. Best-known was the Chisolm Trail, with its southernmost end tapping the lower Río Grande country. Herds from South Texas walked (with occasional stampedes) north to the Red River, across the "Indian Nation" or Oklahoma Territory, and into Kansas. Some went further, as far as Montana and Western Canada. This legendary era, which made the Texas cowboy into a national folk hero, lasted about 20 years. Barbed wire fences, windmills and the building of rail lines into the ranch country itself helped bring the era to a close. By 1890, the old long drives were almost gone, but far from forgotten. They live on in books, movies and television—an indelible part of the South Texas legacy.

As Anglo-Americans, and more than a few African-Americans, took up cattle raising, they adopted the methods, dress and lingo of the experts—the Mexican-Texan *vaqueros*. They learned to ride at a gallop and rope cattle with *la reata*, which became a "lariat;" to gather cattle up in a *rodeo*—later called a round-up—for branding; to be ready to chase a herd seized by a running panic, or *estampida*; to wear leg covers, or *chaparreras*, made of *cuero crudo*, or "raw hide," when riding in thorny brush; and to call themselves vaqueros—which sometimes came out as "buckaroos," or just "cowboys."

Vaquero on trail drive c-1870

Texas Ranger—c. 1870

Lawless conditions gripped South Texas and the border country after the Civil War. Bands of cattle thieves, outlaws and renegades preyed on ranches and villages. Sprawling and isolated, the brushlands offered a refuge for criminals from both sides of the Río Grande. Depredations increased until the citizenry called upon Austin for state help. It soon came with a vengeance, in the form of the Texas Rangers. Led by a former Confederate guerrilla named Leander McNelly, the special force was ordered to "clean up" South Texas, and it did. In 1875-1876, the Rangers swept from Corpus Christi to Brownsville, then upriver to Laredo. Their revolvers and carbines spoke often, exacting a bloody toll from the human predators infesting the region. Unlike local lawmen or the Army, the Rangers crossed into Mexico when they thought it necessary, creating diplomatic problems. On one occasion, McNelly attacked a ranch across the river, said to be a rustlers' den. Only after several innocent Mexicans were killed did the Rangers realize they had the wrong ranch. That incident, along with reports of Ranger mistreatment of Mexicans and Mexican-Texans without apparent cause, stirred fears and hatred among many border Hispanics who felt that the *rinches* themselves were the predators. Fueled by traditional Texan-Mexican animosities dating back to the Alamo and before, the cycle of mutual distrust and hostility continued for many years—sometimes simmering, and at other times flaring up, as during the Mexican Revolution.

Yet many along the Río Grande and in South Texas welcomed the Rangers, and were grateful for their war against the cattle thieves and other outlaws. Praise came from Hispanic and Anglo ranchers, alike, as both groups had been victimized. Despite controversies, Texas Rangers played an ongoing role in border law enforcement for decades. Although much has changed from the old days, the organization still lives, and the Texas Ranger is still regarded as a special breed of peace officer.

Cattle Thieves—c. 1875

"DROP IT!" A South Texas lawman surprises a cattle rustler, caught in the act of "running" or altering a brand. A heated cinch-ring from a saddle could be used to change a brand's appearance. A pair of tongs or crossed sticks could hold the hot ring. Also used was a "running iron"—a straight iron rod with a curve at one end. A cinch ring might not prove a man a rustler, but if caught with a running iron, he was as good as dead. This thief has a quick decision to make—draw, and be shot, or give up—and probably hang.

Widespread cattle stealing plagued South Texas in the late 1800s. Most of the animals were driven across the Río Grande, often for sale to outside buyers. Juan Cortina was said to be rustling from the King and other ranches in the 1870s, and selling the cattle to Cubans. With enormous counties covering vast distances, and county lawmen few, ranchers followed the frontier code—death to rustlers. On occasion, local peace officers caught thieves at work, and if they surrendered, there would be more work for judge and jury.

Cattle thieves - c. - 1875

Rancher's Wife—c. 1880

In the 1880s, as they had since colonial times, women continued their important role in South Texas ranch life. Aside from the usual chores of preparing meals, making and laundering clothes, tending to the sick, educating children, visiting neighbors and aged relatives, and arranging the special celebrations that occurred throughout the year, wives often had the burden of running the ranch while most of the men were away on round-ups or trail drives—sometimes for stretches of several months at a time. They became avid riders, often riding side-saddle to accommodate their long skirts. They managed the ranch hands and workers, keeping daily business running smoothly. Indian attacks, outlaw raids, drought, floods, rattlesnakes, and diseases were all part of the difficult life they faced. But their strength and tenacity saw them through the toughest of times, and their hard work and perseverance blazed a trail for future generations of South Texas ranch families.

Rancher's wife - c. 1880

Breaking a Piñata—c. 1890

In the late 1890s, life in the lower Río Grande region was rich with diversity and ripe for growth and change. New influences from the North, via Anglo settlers and military garrisons along the river, were already changing the cultural landscape. And, of course, the predominant Mexican culture itself was a blend of many other cultures. There was no mistaking the legacies of the ancient Indian way of life, or the strong religious and cultural influences of the Spanish colonization. The influences of the Moors and Jews who came to the New World after their expulsion from Spain in the late 15th century were also there. Even Imperial France's brief rule in Mexico had left its indelible mark on the people of the lower Río Grande.

The resulting culture was a splendid and colorful tapestry—a hybrid that blended the best of all of these influences and came to typify the simple, but festive way of life in the region. Family celebrations were filled with echoes from the cultural melting pot. Children and their families gathered in the shade of mesquite trees to celebrate birthdays and other special occasions with the traditional *papel picado*, or cut paper, and candy-filled *piñatas*—both hold-overs from the Spanish colonization; they enjoyed the brassy sounds of the *mariachi* music that was borne from French wedding music (*les mariages*); they shared culinary treats with indigenous roots, like *tamales;* and dishes with Jewish and Moorish roots, like savory *cabrito,* or goat meat. The seeds of the early settlers had, indeed, taken root, and this once desolate area on the river was beginning to blossom and thrive.

Breaking a Piñata – c. 1890

Stagecoach—c. 1890

For over 50 years, stagecoaches operated along the lower Río Grande. From Mexican War times to the early 1900s, stages linked the region's isolated settlements with one another, and with points north and south, such as Corpus Christi, San Antonio, and Monterrey. Stage travel was often slow and tiresome, but until the railroad came, it was the only public land transportation available. Almost any vehicle with seats could be used as a stage, from light wagons to heavier coaches. Travel in a stagecoach could be quite disagreeable on one of the more spartan models, or relatively comfortable on one of the more elaborate ones.

The stagecoach pictured here was called a "mud wagon." Its baggage rack and window shades made it suitable for passengers who demanded greater comfort in their travel. The well-dressed woman, perhaps the wife of a wealthy merchant, might have frequently traveled in this type of stage—once considered a luxury in this isolated region.

Stagecoach - c. 1890

Plantation Foreman—c. 1895

The farming potential of the lower Río Grande region was recognized long before 1900. Not until the late 1800s, though, did steam-powered irrigation pumps become available to provide the fertile delta lands with enormous quantities of water from the Río Grande. By 1890, several large plantations had sprouted along the river in Cameron and Hidalgo Counties. Hand-dug irrigation ditches carried the water from the river to nearby fields. Harvests were impressive, but without a railroad there was no practical way to ship crops to northern markets in large quantities. Major agricultural development would have to wait a few more years. The pioneer plantations, however, showed the way to the region's future. Here, a foreman oversees a crew at work on an irrigation ditch.

Plantation Foreman - c - 1895

Railroad Construction Gang—c. 1905

A new kind of music rang out along the Río Grande in 1905—the rapid *clang!* of hammers on spikes heralding the arrival of the railroad. While those on Mexico's side had enjoyed rail service for years, the north bank waited until the 20th Century for its turn. Finally, in 1903, the St. Louis, Brownsville and Mexico Railroad began building the line from Robstown southward, reaching Harlingen and Brownsville the next year. West from Harlingen, a spur line snaked across Cameron and Hidalgo counties, accompanied by surveyors, contractors and promoters. With this vital, all-weather link to northern markets, the "flood gates" were open, and development on a big scale was underway.

Like a catalyst, rail transport triggered the practical exploitation of the Río Grande delta's immense agricultural potential. In rolled train-loads of equipment and machinery to build the region's fantastic canal-irrigation systems, and the huge pumps required to send river water to an ever-expanding patchwork of farms. Along the railroad sprang up new towns, to serve as produce and retail centers for farm families and the growing general population. At what must have seemed a break-neck pace, the onrushing 20th Century was changing the old region forever. As ranch life retreated further north, thousands of acres of brush disappeared under cultivation, and before long, the railroad was carrying out an amazing variety of farm products in ever-increasing quantities. Passenger trains also rolled in behind the chugging locomotives; aboard were people eager to get in on the boom—developers, investors, merchants, bankers, salesmen, builders, teachers, and of course, the farmers, many of whom arrived on special "excursion trains" to view new lands and the sales pitches of the land companies. Thus did hundreds, then thousands, come to put down roots and claim a share in the burgeoning growth of the "Rio Grande Valley"—the last frontier of Texas.

Country Doctor—c.1910

Doctors came to this region long before 1900, but for many years they remained scarce. With the development boom of the early 1900s, more physicians were drawn to the region. A familiar figure in those days was the country doctor, yesterday's "general practitioner," who traveled day or night to outlying farms and ranches, bringing modern medicine to those in need. His hallmark was a black leather bag, with the basic instruments and pharmaceuticals he required. A buggy was often his favored means of transport. It carried his bags and other items, and could bring a patient back to town, if necessary. Some doctors retained their buggies well after automobiles appeared, preferring the faithful horse to the uncertainties of the "horseless carriage."

The incoming physicians, with medical school training, were not alone. A centuries-long heritage of herbal and spiritual healing was already in place, handed down from the region's early Native American peoples and Hispanic settlers. Cabeza de Vaca's account tells of the many remedies and treatments which Indians derived from plants, along with supernatural aspects which the native people believed were linked closely with healing. (De Vaca and his companions, in fact, had some rudimentary medical skills, from which a number of their Indian hosts benefitted, qualifying these four wanderers as perhaps the first European doctors in South Texas.) Much later, Escandón's colonists brought their own body of medical knowledge, gleaned from both Spanish and Mexican Indian practices. From these roots came the body of lore known as *curanderismo*, which blends the healing qualities of herbs and other substances with those of the patient's own spirit, under the umbrella of traditional religious beliefs. For many years, the service of a *curandero* was the only medicine available to the region's far-flung rural populace before the country doctor's coming. Even today, folk healing still enjoys a following among the inhabitants of the Rio Grande Valley.

Country Doctor - c. 1905

Real Estate Agent c.1915

The "Magic Valley" was the name given to the lower Río Grande region by its promoters in the early 1900s. "Magic," because its fertile delta soil would grow almost anything, if given enough water. With the coming of the railroad, real estate sales and development took off. Private companies bought up large tracts of land and built irrigation networks to water them. Their sales people, meanwhile, touted the region's benefits and allure in various parts of the U.S., especially the Midwest. Farmers in snow-laden states heard the pitches, and wanted to see for themselves. To accommodate them, the land companies used chartered passenger trains. Hundreds of these trains rolled down into the region from 1910 to around 1930—the heyday of the "land excursion."

The pattern was always the same. At the station the prospective buyers, whom the company called "land seekers" (changed by some wags to "land suckers"), climbed into automobiles and were driven to see modern farms carved from the brushland, complete with houses, barns, sheds, windmills, irrigation ditches—even palm trees and other landscaping. These "model farms" were sales tools to persuade the visiting farmer that what he really wanted most was to leave the snow and ice behind and move to the Magic Valley of the Río Grande. Many hundreds were convinced and bought land right then. When they came back to stay, some found conditions less rosy than promoters had described. "Farms" often were just acres of uncleared, thorny brush, inhabited by rattlesnakes and scorpions. A "farm house" might be a roadside tent. Water supplies were not always reliable, and some irrigation companies went bankrupt. Most, in fact, were later bought by farmers' groups, to ensure a dependable supply. While some newcomers did give up and leave, most others "toughed it out." Their legacy is the region's vast agricultural industry of today.

Real Estate Agent - c. 1915

Mexican Revolutionaries—c. 1915

It was the first great social upheaval of the 20th Century. In 1910, the people of Mexico rose against a dictatorial regime whose policies ensured that the vast majority lived in poverty and near-servitude, had no say in their government, and inherited perpetual debts from their parents. The regime, under the helm of one Porfirio Díaz, thus enabled a small, elite aristocracy to control the country's fortunes, and permitted enormous foreign investment in and domination of Mexico's natural resources and industries. It also denied the equitable distribution of farm and ranch lands to the very *campesinos* who needed it so desperately. The ousting of Díaz and the ascendancy of Madero in 1910 promised long-sought change. But two years later came the enlightened *presidente*'s murder, and the bloody regime of the old *diazista*, Huerta. Years of power struggles, counter-revolts and titanic battles followed, as the nation's very fabric nearly disintegrated. But by the decade's end, the emergence of Obregón as the strongest surviving leader, brought an eventual end to most civil warfare. Not all of the Revolution's goals were achieved, many in Mexico feel its process continues today. But the fiery drama of 1910-1920 did provide the furnace and the anvil with which *los revolucionarios* forged their nation's destiny.

In northeastern Mexico, the Revolution's turmoil surged like a tidal wave against the lower Río Grande boundary, and at times it spilled over. Battles for Reynosa and Matamoros erupted in 1913, and again in 1915. Armed bands of revolutionaries crossed the river to raid Cameron, Willacy, Hidalgo and other counties. Their motives included their need for guns, saddles and supplies, along with the angry desire to settle old scores with *los gringos tejanos*. Gunfire, burnings, killings, and reprisal killings flared across the Magic Valley. These "bandit raids," as the Anglos called them, attracted a veritable army of Texas state troops and National Guardsmen from across the U.S. to protect the border. Tensions rose until another war with Mexico seemed certain by 1916. Then, firmer hands began to gain control of the *revolución*, and tensions eased a bit. Most border troops were soon withdrawn for duty oversees in World War I, and the Revolution's firestorm began to wind down. By 1920 it was almost over, and quiet returned to the Río Grande.

Mexican Revolutionaries - c. 1915

U.S. Army Cavalrymen at a Campsite in the Valley—c. 1916

In 1916, a great many U.S. soldiers came to the lower Río Grande. These were state and National Guard troops, sent to help the "regulars" at the Army posts to secure the border against incursions by Mexican revolutionaries, and, if orders came, to invade Mexico itself. From Port Isabel on the Gulf to San Ygnacio, far upriver, encampments sprang up large and small—along the railroad lines, at pumping stations, at river crossings, at ranches, and in the towns. Long columns of dusty, marching infantry traipsed along roads, while cavalry practiced their maneuvers, and artillery boomed away. Signal Corps men operated telephones, telegraphs, and that new marvel, the "wireless," or radio. They also used another wonder, the aeroplane, in one of its first U.S. military actions. The ominous chatter of machine guns could be heard on firing ranges, joining the single shots of rifles and pistols. Off-duty soldiers visited the growing Valley towns and met the people, sampled the local food (including hot *chiles*), tried speaking Spanish, hunted and fished. They also fought the flies, ants, scorpions, and the chilly winter "northers" that cut right through their heavy tents. On duty, they patrolled the river on horseback and on foot, manning rifle pits which overlooked crossings, guarding the vital irrigation pumping plants, and by their overall presence reassured the Americans on one side, and the Mexicans on the other, that Uncle Sam was on the job and ready to respond.

At times, they did see action, in sporadic fire-fights with *revolucionarios*. Some were wounded, and some died. On at least one occasion, American troopers rode across the Río Grande in pursuit of raiders, engaging them in a shoot-out near Matamoros. A machine-gun unit from Fort Brown also joined the fray, before orders came to withdraw. With U.S.-Mexico tensions high enough already, such an episode could have sparked war. There was no war, however—at least not with Mexico. In the spring of 1917 came the Americans' long-avoided entry into the European conflict. Most of the border troops headed for overseas duty on the Western Front. Reduced forces stayed on border duty, as the worst of Mexico's turmoil ended. But the men of '16-'17 did not forget their border service. Years later, many returned to live in the Rio Grande Valley.

U.S. Army Cavalrymen at a campsite in the Valley - c. 1916

Clearing the Land—c. 1920

Well into the 1900s, the job of land-clearing was done by hand around much of the Valley. Thick and thorny brush—cactus of many types, yucca, agave, native ebony, mesquite—blanketed the region. Railroad lines, farm lands, canal rights-of-way, roads and town sites had to be cleared. Machinery for such work was scarce in the early days, but labor was not. Crews of mostly Hispanic workers attacked brush with hand tools—the *machete*; the *hacha*, or axe; the *legon*, or spade; and the "grubbing hoe" or mattock. The man at right is swinging a mattock, also called an *azuela*. How these men could wade into and remove acres of brush shod only in sandals, and wearing no heavy clothing was a source of wonder to many Anglos. Day after day, for many years, the crews worked, and the brush retreated, making way for fields, as well as citrus groves. By the early 1920s, annual crops of grapefruit and oranges were making the name "Rio Grande Valley" familiar across the United States.

U.S. Cavalrymen, Fort Ringgold—c. 1941

For what would be the last time, U.S. Army horse cavalry patrolled the lower Río Grande during a national emergency. The time was World War II. Over two years after the attack on Pearl Harbor in December 1941, mounted and motorized units of the 124th Cavalry guarded airports, bridges over the river, railroad lines, and other vital points, from possible sabotage. Assigned to the Valley, the troopers were the Army's last horseback soldiers. In 1944, they were ordered overseas, and the Valley forts were closed. A tradition going back to the Mexican War thus came to an honorable close. Turning in its last horses, the 124th later found itself in the jungles and mountains of Burma, fighting as infantry against the Japanese in 1944-45. They were still in the China-Burma-India theater (CBI) when the war ended in August, 1945.

The 124th was organized as a Texas State Guard cavalry regiment in 1929, and became a Federal outfit in 1940, as the nation began to mobilize for possible war. Attached to the Army's First Cavalry Division, the 124th had a squadron and Regimental Headquarters at Fort Brown, with a second squadron at Fort Ringgold, near Rio Grande City. Fort Ringgold is the setting of this picture, with the arches of the old post hospital as a backdrop. An Army nurse offers a cigarette to a mounted officer of the "1st Cav," its distinctive yellow-shield patch on his sleeve. A drill instructor looks on, at right.

Both Fort Ringgold and Fort Brown later became educational institutions—a transformation that symbolized the changes brought to the whole region by the Second World War. In 1941, it was still isolated, with a way of life that had changed very little since the 1800s. By the late 1940s, it was inextricably bound to every other part of the state, the nation, and increasingly, the world, through advances in communication and transportation—especially television and air travel. With WWII, an entire epoch of frontier isolation, stretching back over centuries, began to fade. From the Paleo-Indian dawn to the horse cavalry's sunset, it is the story we have told here—the story of the lower Río Grande borderlands.

U.S. Cavalrymen, Fort Ringgold, c. 1941

Index of Illustrations

	Page
Map: The Lower Río Grande of Southern Texas and Northeastern Mexico .... (1994)	17
Paleo Indian Hunters, c.8000 B.C. .... (1985)	45
Northern Mexico Indian Traders at El Sal del Rey Lake, c.1400 .... (1993)	47
Coahuiltecan Indian, c.1500 .... (1985)	49
Spanish Conquistadors at Rio de las Palmas, c.1520 .... (1985)	51
Cabeza de Vaca in Southern Texas, c.1535 .... (1996)	53
"English Wanderers" on Texas Soil, c.1570 .... (1996)	55
Don Luis de Carvajal, c.1585 .... (1995)	57
Dutch Intruders on the Lower Río Grande, c.1630 .... (1996)	59
Ganadero Español del Nuevo Reino de León, c.1650 .... (1985)	61
Sargento Mayor Alonso de León's Expedition, c.1687 .... (1993)	63
Cattle Coming into Texas, c.1690 .... (1985)	65
El Exmo. Sr. Don Joseph de Escandón y Elguera, c.1749 .... (1981)	67
"Pobladores" with Escandón, c.1750 .... (1985)	69
Vaquero de Nuevo Santander, c.1750 .... (1980)	71
Taking Formal Possession of Land, c.1760 .... (1995)	73
Surveyors - Upper Valley Region, c.1767 .... (1985)	75
Spanish Colonial Frontier Dragoons on Patrol in Nuevo Santander, c.1770 .... (1993)	77
Spanish Colonial-era Cattle Drive, c.1776 .... (1996)	79
Spanish Colonial-era "Mesteñeros", c.1780 .... (1996)	81
Caporal (Cowboys' Foreman), c.1780 .... (1985)	83
Salt Miners–"salineros"–at El Sal del Rey Lake, c.1790 .... (1985)	85
Franciscan Visiting Upper Valley Settlements, c.1800 .... (1985)	87
Colonial Sheep Herder and Family, c.1800 .... (1996)	89
Frontier Hispanic Family Defending Their Home, c.1810 .... (1996)	91
Lipan Apache Warriors, c.1820 .... (1985)	93
Mexican "Insurgentes"–Independence Fighters–on the Northern Frontier, c.1820 ... (1993)	95
"Ganadero" and "Vaquero" - Mid-Valley Area, c.1830 .... (1985)	97
Texan Adventurers (Filibusters), c.1840 .... (1985)	99
Zachary Taylor's U.S. Army Dragoon Talking to Sarah Borginnis, c.1846 .... (1993)	101
Mexican Cavalrymen at the Battle of Buena Vista, c.1847 .... (1993)	103
Steamboat Captain, c.1850 .... (1986)	105
U.S. Army Lt. at Fort Ringgold, c.1851 .... (1985)	107
Blacksmith, Ranch Settlement, c.1860 .... (1985)	109
Juan Nepomuceno Cortina's Raiders, c.1860 .... (1993)	111
Cotton Trade During the Civil War, c.1863 .... (1993)	113
Confederate Camels at Brownsville, c.1864 .... (1993)	115
Union Army Soldiers at Palmito Ranch, Last Battle of the Civil War, c.1865 .... (1993)	117
Confederate Army Soldiers at the Battle of Palmito Ranch, c.1865 .... (1993)	119
The New Beginning .... (1984)	121
French Imperial Forces Along the Río Grande, c.1865 .... (1996)	123
Mexican Soldiers, c.1865 .... (1996)	125
Vaquero on Trail Drive, c.1870 .... (1985)	127
Texas Ranger, c.1870 .... (1985)	129
Cattle Thieves, c.1875 .... (1985)	131
Rancher's Wife, c.1880 .... (1986)	133
Breaking a Piñata, c.1890 .... (1995)	135
Stagecoach, c.1890 .... (1985)	137
Plantation Foreman, c.1895 .... (1985)	139
Railroad Construction Gang, c.1905 .... (1985)	141
Country Doctor, c.1905 .... (1986)	143
Real Estate Agent, c.1915 .... (1985)	145
Mexican Revolutionaries, c.1915 .... (1993)	147
U.S. Army Cavalrymen at a Campsite in the Valley, c.1916 .... (1993)	149
Clearing the Land, c.1920 .... (1998)	151
U.S. Cavalrymen, Fort Ringgold, c.1941 .... (1993)	153

Original illustrations measure approximately 20 inches deep by 15 inches wide, including a wide margin of several inches on all sides. Most are rendered on illustration board using a combination of pen-and-ink and colored pencil.

Suggested Reading

Almaráz, Félix D. (Felix Diaz), *Tragic Cavalier; Governor Manuel Salcedo of Texas.* College Station: Texas A&M University Press, 1971.

Alonzo, Amando C., *Tejano Legacy: Rancheros and Settlers in South Texas, 1734-1900.* Albuquerque: University of New Mexico Press, 1998.

Bauer, K. Jack, *The Mexican War, 1846-1848.* New York: Macmillian and Company, 1947.

Cabeza de Vaca, Alvár Nuñez, *Adventures in the Unknown Interior of America.* Albuquerque: University of New Mexico Press, 1992.

Chamberlain, Samuel E., *My Confession: The Recollections of a Rogue.* Lincoln: University of Nebraska Press, 1987.

Chipman, Donald E., *Spanish Texas, 1519-1821.* Austin: University of Texas Press, 1992.

Cisneros, José, *Riders Across the Centuries: Horsemen of the Spanish Borderlands.* El Paso: Texas Western Press, 1984.

Durham, George, *Taming the Nueces Strip: The Story of McNelly's Rangers.* Austin: University of Texas Press, 1994.

Hester, Thomas R., *Digging into South Texas Prehistory: A Guide for Amateur Archaeologists.* San Antonio: Corona Publishing Company, 1980.

Hill, Lawrence F., *José de Escandón and the Founding of Nuevo Santander.* Columbus: Ohio State University Press, 1926.

Horgan, Paul, *Great River: The Rio Grande in North American History.* New York: Rhinehart & Company, 1954.

Kelley, Pat, *River of Lost Dreams: Navigation on the Rio Grande.* Lincoln: University of Nebraska Press, 1986.

Miller, Hubert J., *José de Escandón, Colonizer of Nuevo Santander.* Edinburg, Texas: New Santander Press, 1980.

Newcomb, W. W., Jr., *The Indians of Texas from Prehistoric to Modern Times.* Austin: University of Texas Press, 1994.

Robertson, Brian, *Wild Horse Desert: The Heritage of South Texas.* Edinburg, Texas: Hidalgo County Historical Museum, 1985.

Salinas, Martín, *Indians on the Rio Grande Delta: Their Role in the History of Southern Texas and Northeastern Mexico.* Austin: University of Texas Press, 1961.

Sánchez, Mario L., *A Shared Experience: The History, Architecture and Historic Designations of the Lower Rio Grande Heritage Corridor.* Austin: Los Caminos del Río Heritage Project and the Texas Historical Commission, 1991.

Sandos, James A., *Rebellion in the Borderlands: Anarchism and the Plan of San Diego 1904- 1923.* Norman: University of Oklahoma Press, 1992.

Scott, Florence Johnson. *Historical Heritage of the Lower Rio Grande.* Waco: Texian Press, 1966.

Stambaugh, J. Lee, *The Lower Rio Grande Valley of Texas: Its Colonization and Industrialization 1518-1953.* Austin: Jenkins Publishing Company, 1954.

Thomas, Hugh, *Conquest: Montezuma, Cortés, and the Fall of Old México.* New York: Simon & Schuster (Touchstone), 1993.

Thompson, Jerry Don, *A Wild and Vivid Land: An Illustrated History of the South Texas Border.* Austin: Texas State Historical Association, 1997.

Thompson, Jerry Don, ed., *Fifty Miles and a Fight: Major Samuel Heintzelman's Journal of Texas and the Cortina War.* Austin: Texas State Historical Association, 1998.

Trudeau, Noah A., *Like Men of War: Black Troops in the Civil War 1862-1865.* New York: Little, Brown & Company, 1998.

Vielé, Therese G., *Following the Drum: A Glimpse of Frontier Life.* Lincoln: University of Nebraska Press, 1984.

Wallace, Ernest, David Vigness and George Ward. *Documents of Texas History,* 2nd ed. Austin: State House Press, 1992.

Weddle, Robert S., *The French Thorn: Rival Explorers in the Spanish Seas, 1682-1762.* College Station: Texas A&M University Press, 1991.

Acknowledgements

ARTWORK BY

José Cisneros, *HCHM Collection*

AUTHORS

Dr. Félix D. Almaráz, Jr.
Dr. Hubert J. Miller

PICTURE TEXTS

Tom Fort, *Staff*
Rachael Freyman, *Staff*

EDITOR

Jackie Nirenberg, *Staff*

DESIGN

Erren Seale, *Design & Production*
Fernando Rivera, *Production Assistant*

COLOR WORK / PRINT COORDINATION

Bob Carter

HCHM PUBLICATIONS COMMITTEE

Monica Zárate Burdette, *Chairman*
Evelyn East
Mary Lary
Ray Stafford
Sandra Thomas
Joan Jones
Carol Lynn Looney, *Ex-Officio*
Jackie Nirenberg, *Staff*

Preserving Our Borderland Heritage

In the mid 1960s, a group of visionaries from the area met in Edinburg, Texas and committed themselves to preserving the remarkable history of the lower Río Grande region. Their dream was to build a world-class museum—an historical center that could preserve borderland heritage for generations to come. In 1970, their dream became a reality when the Hidalgo County Historical Museum opened its doors to the public. Since then, the Museum has aspired to fulfill a mission: "to preserve and present the borderland heritage of South Texas and northeastern Mexico." It continues to do so by collecting and preserving artifacts, maintaining an extensive regional archive, mounting exhibitions based on original research, providing educational programming, and producing award-winning publications.

Hidalgo County Historical Museum

1998 BOARD OF TRUSTEES

Carol Lynn Looney, *Chairman*
Laurie Lozano, *Chairman-Elect*
Cole Abbott, *Vice-Chairman*
Joe Brown, *Treasurer*
Esther Jenkins, *Secretary*
Cayetano Barrera
Providence Boneta
Jerry Box
Kathy Collins
Monica Zárate Burdette
Jane Cozad
Sam de la Garza
Mark Dizdar
Evelyn East
Mariella Gorena
Maxine Guerra
Tim Havens
Sonia Perez
Bill Robertson
Jabier Rodriguez
Adela Staretz
Kurt Stephen
Sandra Thomas
Lisa Wallace

121 E. McIntyre
Edinburg, Texas 78539
(956) 383-6911
FAX (956) 381-8518

ADVISORY COUNCIL

Tony Aguirre
Susan Barbee
Carolyn Bell
Danny Butler
Dardanella Cardenas
Foss Jones
Lan Jones
Mary Lary
Frances McAllen
Ray Stafford

STAFF

Shan Rankin, *Executive Director*
Tom Fort, *Assistant Director / Curator of Exhibits*
David Mycue, *Curator of Archives & Collections*
Lynne Beeching, *Development Officer*
Rachael Freyman, *Education Officer*
Jackie Nirenberg, *Public Relations Officer*
Marisela Saenz, *Administrative Assistant*
Robert García, *Receptionist / Office Clerk*
Joe Hernandez, *Building Supervisor*
Delfina Lopez, *Collections Clerk*
Jose Francisco Garza, *Maintenance*